PITCHING
The Keys to Excellence

Sports Illustrated Winner's Circle Books

BOOKS ON TEAM SPORTS

Baseball
Football: Winning Defense
Football: Winning Offense
Hockey
Lacrosse
Pitching

BOOKS ON INDIVIDUAL SPORTS

Bowling
Competitive Swimming
Golf
Racquetball
Skiing
Tennis
Track: Championship Running

SPECIAL BOOKS

Canoeing
Fly Fishing
Scuba Diving
Strength Training

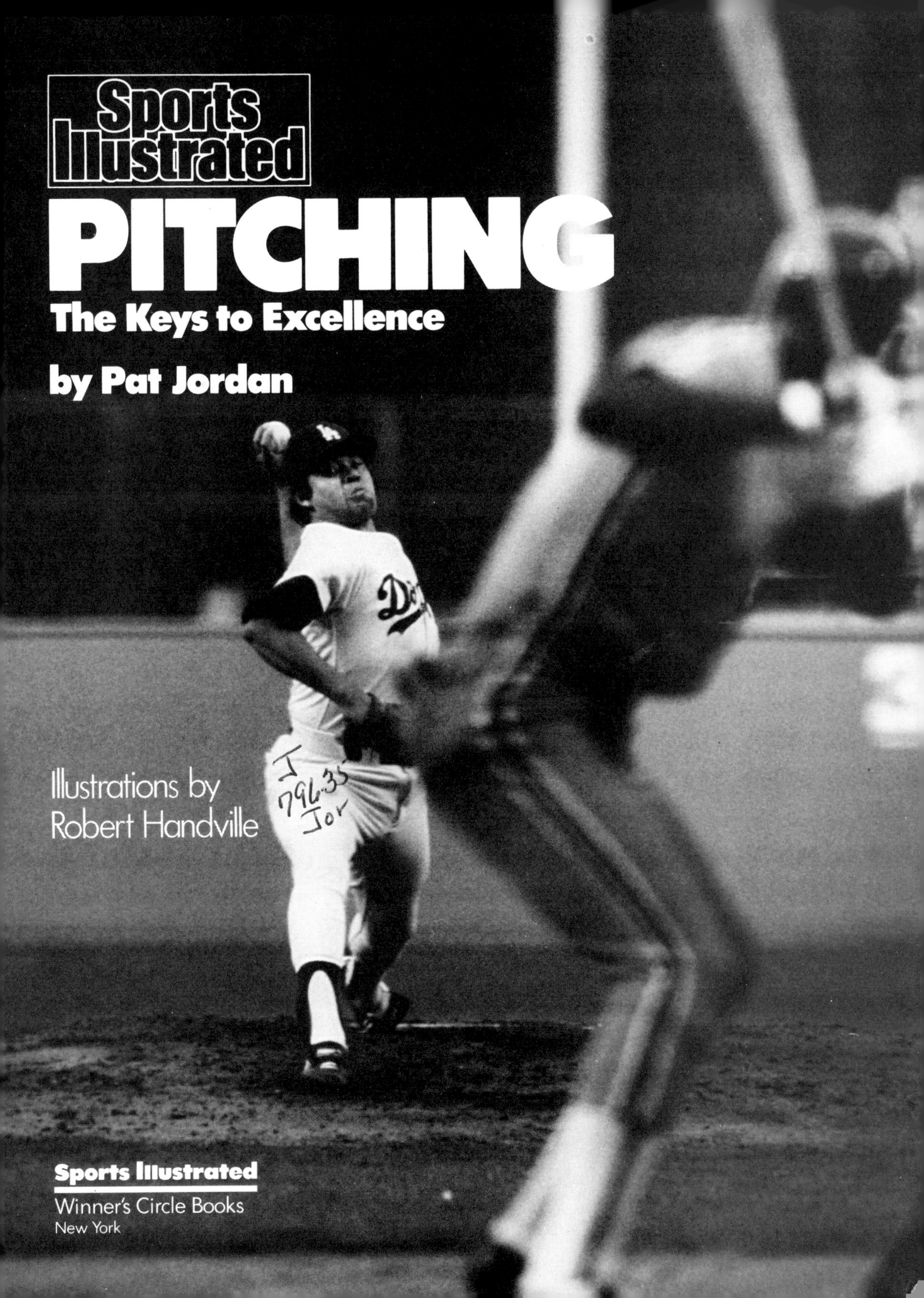

Sports Illustrated

PITCHING

The Keys to Excellence

by Pat Jordan

Illustrations by
Robert Handville

I
796.33
Jor

Sports Illustrated
Winner's Circle Books
New York

Photo credits: p. 8—courtesy of the Chicago White Sox; p. 37—Stan Wayman, *Life* magazine, © Time Inc; for *Sports Illustrated*: pp. 58, 100, 116—John Iacono; pp. 35, 58, 62, 96, 112, 124—Walter Iooss, Jr.; pp. 57, 110, 124—Bill Smith; p. 108—Manny Millan; p. 118—Bill Jaspersohn; p. 117—Heinz Kluetmeier; p. 14—Neil Leifer; p. 3—Peter Read Miller; pp. 12, 56, 75—Ronald C. Modra; p. 11—Mickey Pfleger; p. 139—V.J. Lovero; p. 20—Chuck Solomon; p. 106—Tony Tomsic; pp. 66, 78—Tony Tomsic.

All illustrations by Robert Handville.

Library of Congress Cataloging-in-Publication Data

Jordan, Pat.
  Sports illustrated pitching.

  Summary: Explains the basics of pitching and proper techniques for throwing the fastball, curveball, slider, screwball, knuckleball, and others.
    1. Pitching (Baseball) [1. Pitching (Baseball) 2. Baseball] I. Handville, Robert, ill.
II. Sports illustrated (Time, inc.) III. Title. IV. Title: Pitching.
GV871.J67 1988   796.357'22   87-35639
ISBN 0-452-26101-5 (pbk.)   88 88 90 91 92 AG/HL 10 9 8 7 6 5 4 3 2 1

Contents

PITCHING
The Keys to Excellence

Introduction

Not every youth can become a Sandy Koufax or a Tom Seaver, but every youth can become a pitcher—and a modestly successful one at that. It is the difference between a craftsman and an artist; the former can be taught, while the latter requires a special gift. To be a great pitcher, like Seaver was, one must have a superior arm and a great fastball. But over the years there have been numerous successful pitchers—Whitey Ford, for example—who have been able to compensate for a modest fastball by developing a keen pitcher's intelligence, a smooth, deceptive delivery, pinpoint control, and a wide assortment of off-speed and breaking pitches. All of these attributes can be taught to any modestly talented, willing, and intelligent youth. You *can* learn how to pitch! Your success might be limited to high-school baseball or maybe to Babe Ruth American Legion baseball or —perhaps even collegiate baseball, or baseball as advanced as the minor leagues. But still, with practice, you will have experienced not only some of the joys of pitching but—even better—some of the thrill of pitching right.

Young pitchers, especially preteens, should concentrate on three aspects of their craft. First and most important, they should learn to throw

9

Tom Seaver displays the classic motion that helped make him one of the game's outstanding pitchers.

the ball with a natural and proper motion. This includes both their arm motion and their pitching delivery (pump, kick, follow-through, and so forth). A pitcher's motion is like the foundation of an elaborately constructed mansion. No matter how expensive the interior paneling may be, that mansion will be a failure if its foundation is flawed. The same is true with a pitcher's motion. It is what leads him to his best fastball, sharpest curve, and finest control. It is the foundation on which every single aspect of his craft rests. No matter how much a pitcher sweats and strains, he will never develop his best fastball unless he first develops his proper motion.

Second, as a young pitcher you should try to develop strength in your arm so that you can throw your best and most natural fastball. You should, as quickly as possible, reach the limits of your natural talent. The secret of pitching is to develop a good fastball first, and only later, for the times when the fastball will be insufficient, to develop other, less natural pitches, like the curveball. A young pitcher should throw only fastballs until his teenage years. At that point he can begin work on other pitches.

There are two dangers in a young pitcher throwing curveballs too soon: it could damage his arm, and it could take away speed from his developing fastball. Damage can occur when the pitcher begins throwing a curveball with an incorrect motion, an easy habit to fall into when young. On the other hand, a properly thrown curveball puts *less* strain on a pitcher's arm than a properly thrown fastball, since a curveball motion is more natural than a fastball motion. And since there is less strain, the arm will remain weaker, more undeveloped than if the pitcher were throwing mostly fastballs.

The third basic of pitching is control. While the young pitcher is developing his motion and speed, he should simultaneously be developing his control —i.e., his ability to throw the ball over any part of the plate. All three basics are intertwined so that the development of any one leads to the advancement of the others. The more naturally you throw the ball, the faster your pitch will be and the easier your ability to control it.

If there is a fourth basic to pitching, it is a basic so intangible that it cannot really be taught. With time and pitching experience, you should develop what is commonly called "savvy," which is really a pitcher's intelligence. Some say it is instinct. Others claim that savvy can be learned, that all it requires is a modestly intelligent, willing, and attentive mind. Whichever is true, only time will tell, and the best you can do is to remain mentally alert and receptive to experience whenever you are on the mound. For example, when a batter takes such a hard swing at your pitch that he pulls your best fastball into foul territory, your intelligence should tell you that he will miss a slower pitch—so throw one.

The only way to develop all three (or four) basics of pitching is by pitching. There are no drills or calisthenics that can develop these basics as quickly, as properly, and as naturally as the simple act of pitching a baseball. However, you cannot pitch a game every day, nor should you throw a ball every day. The strain on your arm would be too great. At most, a young pitcher should pitch no more than two games a week, and should throw a baseball (i.e., warm-up and/or game) no more than four times a week. The ideal throwing schedule is to warm up two days before you pitch in a game, and then to warm up two days after. In between these bouts of throwing, you should not put any strain on your arm. This does not mean you can't "soft-toss" a leisurely game of catch, but even in this soft-tossing you should concentrate on your craft of throwing a ball, no matter how easily, with the proper motion. A pitcher should always throw like a pitcher, even when playing catch with an infielder. His every baseball moment should be designed to practice his natural pitching delivery until it no longer becomes a thing learned but simply a natural extension of himself, like walking.

Even when tossing on the sidelines, smart pitchers always throw with the proper motion.

Warming up, an art in itself, can determine a pitcher's success, or lack of it, in any given game. The proper way to warm up before a game is to begin by taking a light run around the park to loosen your muscles and get the adrenaline flowing; then, after a light set of calisthenics (e.g., touching toes, jumping jacks, sit-ups), you should start throwing to the catcher from a distance of, say, 45 feet—assuming you intend to pitch from the regulation major-league distance of 60 feet 6 inches. This "short throwing" is more for psychological ease than anything else, and you should advance to the regulation distance as quickly as possible. On each successive pitch you should extend your arm farther. A sustained period of soft lobs accomplishes nothing. Conversely, throwing your best fastball before you are sufficiently warmed up can damage your arm. Only after you have advanced to your best fastball and have thrown about eight of them should you begin lofting slow curveballs until, again, you are throwing your hardest curveball.

At this point the pitcher should begin to mix up his pitches—fastball, curveball, fastball, and so forth—just as he would in a game. He should finish his warm-ups ten to fifteen minutes after he has started throwing. To throw longer than fifteen minutes will tire a pitcher out before he even takes the mound, and to throw less than ten minutes will risk the possibility of injuring an insufficiently loosened-up arm.

Waiting to start a game, and between innings of a game, the pitcher should keep his arm warm. He should never expose it to an air-conditioned room or a cold wind. However, after he has finished pitching, he should pack his shoulder in ice for about ten minutes to alleviate the swelling caused by the strain put on his arm during the game.

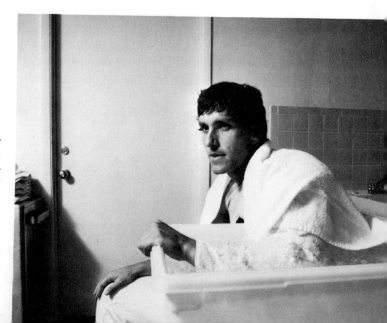

To reduce swelling and minimize stiffness after pitching a game, most major-league pitchers soak the arm in ice water for about ten minutes.

On off days when a pitcher is not throwing—even on days when he will merely warm up—he should undertake a routine of calisthenics and running designed both to loosen the muscles in his limbs, back, and shoulders and to strengthen the muscles in his legs. A pitcher's legs are almost as important to his pitching as his arm is. They must sustain the strenuous effort of pushing off the rubber for more than one hundred pitches a game.

Throwing a baseball is a stretching, reaching motion that requires elastic, loose muscles, and calisthenics should include a variety of muscle-stretching and -loosening routines. Sit-ups, toe touching, jumping jacks, and so forth are excellent for this purpose. On the other hand, routines that tighten and constrict a pitcher's muscles, such as push-ups and weight lifting, are less helpful and are sometimes even harmful—although in some isolated cases, weight lifting can be beneficial. If a pitcher's arm is basically weak or if he is recovering from a sore arm, then weight lifting can help. But in general, a young pitcher should avoid weight lifting until well into his teens, when he will better know whether or not he will need its special benefits.

For running exercises, you will get more benefit from short, all-out sprints than you will from leisurely jogging. Jogging will loosen up a pitcher's legs, but short sprints will develop leg power, and strong legs are what sustain a pitcher over a long game. A good sprinting routine is to run full speed for 100 yards, walk 50 yards, run 100 yards, and so on for about ten to twenty sprints a day. But remember: Running and calisthenics are merely peripheral aids to throwing a baseball. No amount of either can be anywhere nearly as beneficial as the simple act of throwing. The only way anyone can become a pitcher is to pitch.

1

The Motion

All successful pitchers succeed for the same reason. They throw the ball with a smooth and classically correct motion. Such a motion is the common denominator which, over the years, has separated the Tom Seavers, Jim Palmers, Sandy Koufaxes, and Nolan Ryans from their less successful brethren. Granted, the motions of each of these great pitchers contain certain idiosyncrasies, but they all contain the same basic pitching mechanics, are all part of a carefully constructed routine whose purpose is to produce the maximum effort. A pitcher's motion is like an auto engine. Both contain a dozen revolving and pumping parts, all of which help build up power and rhythm that propel the ball—or the car—in a particular direction at a particular speed. A proper pitching motion will help the pitcher throw the ball with his maximum strength, will help him throw the ball in a desired direction, will put the least amount of strain on his arm (a fragile limb never designed for the steady throwing of a baseball) and, finally, will help him deceive his opponent, the batter.

Let me define and illustrate proper pitching mechanics. Our subject pitcher will be a right-

15

Sandy Koufax, one of the greatest pitchers of all time, was known for his blazing fastball and flawless delivery.

handed thrower, although the same rules will apply equally (although conversely) to left-handed throwers.

THE MECHANICS OF GOOD MOTION

The Stance

The purpose of a proper stance on the rubber is to give the pitcher correct balance before he begins his elaborate motion, in order to make sure his weight is properly distributed in preparation for the shifting back and forth which occurs throughout a pitcher's delivery.

With no runners on base, the pitcher takes his sign from the catcher with his right foot bisecting the rubber and pointing toward the catcher. His left foot should be a few inches behind and to the left of his right foot. The left leg should be slightly flexed so that most of the pitcher's weight is forward on his right leg, as if he is already about to explode toward the batter. The pitcher can take his sign in either of two ways: with his glove hand at his side and his ball hand

The Stance.
The right-handed pitcher's right foot rests on the center of the rubber and the left foot remains behind.

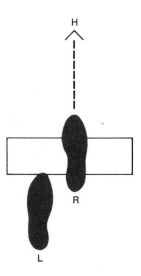

behind his back, or with his ball hand and glove hand joined in front at his waist as if in prayer. The purpose of both positions is to conceal his grip on the ball so that the batter will not be able to tell what kind of pitch will be coming.

The Stance

The pitcher's weight is forward on his right leg and his left leg is slightly flexed.

18

The Pump

A   B

As the pitcher's hands rise, his weight shifts back onto his left leg (A). Then, as his forward motion begins, his right foot turns parallel to the rubber (B).

The Pump

The pitcher's pump helps to build the proper rhythm from which most good pitchers obtain much of their power. It also helps to position the pitcher's foot securely against the rubber so that he can push off with his maximum force toward the plate.

The pitcher begins his motion with his hands joined at his waist. As both hands rise in front of his eyes, his weight shifts from his right foot back to his left foot so that he appears to be leaning back away from the batter. When his hands are almost fully extended (and still joined) above his head, almost all his weight will be resting on his still flexed left leg, while his right foot is only lightly touching the rubber. In this position the pitcher slides his right foot off the rubber by turning it parallel to the rubber—toe facing third base—and then sliding it forward into the indentation in the dirt that is always found in front of a pitching rubber on a mound. His position now resembles that of a fencer about to spring forward on the attack.

A   B   C

In the no-windup delivery, the pitcher begins with his weight forward on his right leg and his left leg slightly flexed, as in the pump delivery (A). But then, after pivoting on the rubber with his right foot (B), he raises his left leg until his thigh is parallel to the ground, but he does not lift his arms over his head (C).

Note: Some very successful pitchers, notably Dave Righetti of the Yankees, avoid a pump entirely in their delivery. They simply place their glove hand and ball hand at their waist and then go immediately from there into their kick. The reasoning behind the no-pump delivery is that the less motion in a delivery, the easier will it be for a pitcher to control his pitches. A lot of hard-throwing pitchers with control problems, like Righetti, have resorted to this no-pump delivery over the years. It has helped some gain much needed control while causing only a slight loss in speed. However, it is not the ideal delivery. The

Some pitchers, like Dave Righetti of the Yankees, feel that not winding up gives them a more compact, efficient delivery. Maybe so. But the pump helps ensure a critical ingredient when pitching: rhythm.

ideal delivery should begin with a full pump in order to build up a rhythm that will add a few miles per hour to one's fastball, not take a few miles per hour away from it. A pitcher's primary goal is to get the best out of his arm and then, secondarily, to try to control it. Anything else is a compromise, an attempt to mute a blazing talent for quick and sometimes transitory success.

The Kick

The purpose of the kick is to shift the weight backward toward second base, in such a way that the pitcher still retains his balance but also builds up a kind of rocking back-and-forth rhythm that eventually will evolve into a physical explosion toward the plate.

The pitcher's weight now moves forward onto his right foot, and as it does, his left foot leaves the ground. His body swivels from left to right toward third base, his left leg rising as he swivels, until he has turned himself completely sideways to the batter. At this point he resembles a crane standing on one leg in a swamp. All his weight is now on his right foot. His left leg is raised and bent at a level with his waist. His hands above his head are just beginning their descent toward his bent left leg. If properly executed, this position can be held indefinitely in a state of perfect balance. If at this point a pitcher finds himself

The Crane Position

The kick begins with the pitcher's weight balanced on his right foot, his left leg raised. His arms begin their downward motion.

Improper Balance

In (A) the pitcher's weight is too far forward. In (B) his weight is too far back.

A

B

falling forward toward third base, then his weight is not perpendicular to the
rubber as it should be. The result will be a pitch that crosses the plate inside
and high to a right-handed batter. The opposite is true if he finds himself falling
backward toward first base. The result will be a pitch far on the outside to a
right-handed batter. Meanwhile, his hands have simultaneously moved down
toward his bent leg. Just before they touch the raised knee, the two hands
separate. The glove hand falls on the home-plate side of the raised knee and
the ball hand falls on the second-base side of the knee and begins to move back
and down toward second base. It is important for the pitcher's ball hand to
move directly toward second base. If it swings back too far toward first base,
the pitcher will be in a "locked" position, and his body rhythm will be out of
sync, so that when his body moves forward toward the plate, his arm, instead
of moving toward the plate simultaneously, will follow much later.

Still standing like a crane, the pitcher now shifts his weight slightly back
toward second base, as if his ball hand were trying to reach back to touch the
base. Again, if the pitcher reaches too far back he will lose the balance that is

The Windup

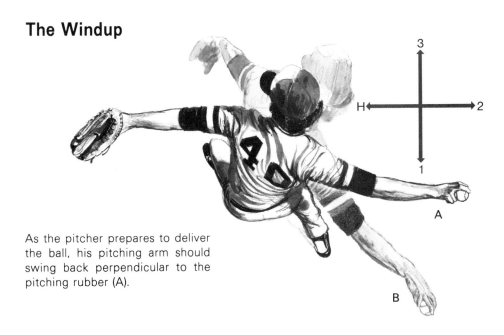

As the pitcher prepares to deliver
the ball, his pitching arm should
swing back perpendicular to the
pitching rubber (A).

(B) Wrong! The pitcher's body is
overrotated and "locked," wasting
valuable momentum.

Hip Tilt

2nd

The kick out begins from a balanced position, hips tilted toward second, pitching arm reaching down and back toward second base.

The Kick

(A) The pitcher's left leg kicks out and swings forward toward home.

(B) Momentum is developed as the body rotates, following the left leg.

(C) As the left foot lands in the stride position, it pulls the body forward. This, along with the simultaneous pushing action of the right foot, produces much of the pitcher's power.

A

B

C

so essential to good pitching. His hips should be tilted in such a way that his left hip facing the plate is higher than his right hip facing second base.

Next, the pitcher begins his spring forward toward the batter. His arm and all his weight explode simultaneously toward the batter. His raised left leg kicks out at a point halfway between home plate and third base and then swings from right to left toward the plate. His hips swivel from right to left, and as his left leg pulls his body toward the plate, his right foot, firmly placed against the rubber, simultaneously pushes off the rubber toward the plate. Much of a pitcher's power comes from the combined force of the left leg's kick toward the plate and the right leg's thrust off the rubber. This power smoothly catapults his entire body toward the batter and, almost as much as his arm, is responsible for the speed of his fastball. It is for this most important push that the great pitchers like Seaver, Koufax, Ryan, *et. al.*, work so hard at strengthening their calves and thighs.

The Stride

As much as any part of his delivery, a pitcher's stride will determine where the ball will be thrown. The length and position of that stride will directly influence a pitcher's control and is often the first part of his motion that he must alter in order to change the direction of his pitches.

As the left leg is swinging from third base toward the plate, the pitcher's arm is simultaneously moving forward (with the rest of his body) from second base. When the pitcher's left foot comes down on the dirt, his right arm should be passing alongside his head. At this point the pitcher's legs are spread apart about as far as possible. He is very low to the ground. All his weight from the waist up is lunging forward toward the batter. His left leg is bent, and his left foot is planted firmly in the dirt for balance and pulling power; it literally grips the dirt like a claw and pulls the pitcher forward. His right leg is stretched backward in an almost direct line with the rest of his body—his right foot still in contact with the rubber.

As the pitcher releases the ball at a point about 12 inches in front of his head, his right foot leaves the rubber and his right leg swings up—about as high as his waist—before it comes down toward the plate. Even after he has released the ball, the pitcher's arm still continues its flight toward the plate in conjunction with his swinging right leg. When the right leg is finally down and the right foot touches the dirt, it should touch at a point parallel to or a few inches ahead of the left foot, with the feet 18 to 24 inches apart.

The Stride

In the full-stride position, the pitcher's legs are far apart, his upper body has lunged forward, and his throwing arm is moving past his head.

The Release

As the ball is released, the pitcher's right leg leaves the rubber and swings up and forward. The throwing arm continues its proper motion toward the plate.

The Follow-Through

Like the stride, the follow-through will help determine a pitcher's control and, if properly executed, will give a bit of additional speed to his pitch by carrying him forward toward the batter. It will also give the pitcher the proper balance needed to field balls hit back through the mound.

The pitcher's arm should continue forward, passing in front of his chest and down until it comes to rest at a point about 2 inches to the left of his left ankle. The pitcher is now bent well over, his face staring at the ground, with all the weight of his body centered on his left leg and foot. The right foot should be merely touching the ground lightly for balance—to keep him from falling over. From their original starting position on the rubber, the pitcher's feet should be in the following position: his left foot should be about 4 feet in front

Proper Follow-Through

WEIGHT

The pitcher's arm travels forward and down across his chest, coming to rest near his left ankle. The pitcher's body is bent over, the weight on the left leg. Throughout the entire motion (save, perhaps, for an instant or two in the early stages of the windup), his eyes are on the target, the catcher's glove.

The Follow-Through: Correct Foot Position

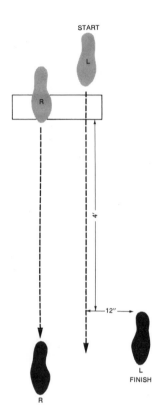

of the rubber (depending on the length of the pitcher's stride and of his legs) and about 12 inches to the left of its starting point. His right foot should also be about 4 feet in front of its starting point; however, it should be straight ahead. In other words, the pitcher's legs are now considerably more spread apart than when he began his motion on the rubber. This is called "opening up," and it greatly affects a pitcher's speed and control.

COMMON ERRORS

What passes for pitching genius—and what often separates great pitchers from good pitchers—is a pitcher's ability to pick up his own pitching errors either during or immediately after the throwing of a pitch. Tom Seaver, for example, was his own best coach. He could tell immediately after he had thrown a high curveball, for instance, what he had done wrong in his motion to make that curveball go high, and then what he should do to correct the error. And, of course, he had the physical and mental talent to correct it on his next pitch. However, the rest of us mortals may not be so gifted. The best we can hope for is to have an intelligent pitching coach who will help us spot such errors in our delivery, which we, caught up in the moment, cannot see. Pitching errors occur generally when a pitcher's concentration slips and he forgets to execute part of his motion properly; when he is physically weak or tired; or when his motion is flawed or insufficiently developed. The best way to avoid errors in pitching is by correcting them while pitching or warming up. No amount of "trick drills" will help a pitcher perfect his motion or break bad habits better than the simple act of pitching.

One of the most common errors made by young pitchers is called "rush-

Rushing

Power is lost when the pitcher lets his body weight and motion get too far ahead of his throwing arm.

ing." This occurs when the pitcher should be in the crane position facing third base but has swung his left leg too far back toward shortstop which in turn has pulled his right arm too far toward first base instead of back toward second base. At this point a pitcher has almost turned his back on the batter. When the pitcher begins to move forward in this rushing position, two things happen that will affect his speed and control. First, his legs and body will be moving ahead of his arm, and second, his rhythm will be out of sync. His body weight will not be helping his arm speed but will be so far ahead of it that he is just throwing or flinging the ball with his arm without benefit of his body motion. Usually his left foot will land on the ground before his right arm passes alongside his head, rather than at the same moment. With his rhythm spent, his right arm will swing forward all by itself, greatly lessening the speed of the pitch.

Another error common among young pitchers is failing to open up—that is, the pitcher does not pull his left leg far enough to the left during his stride and follow-through. This stems from a lazy or weak left leg. The left foot, instead of landing 12 inches or so to the left of its starting point, lands in a direct line with or maybe even to the right of its starting point. This means that his

Failure to Open Up: Foot Position

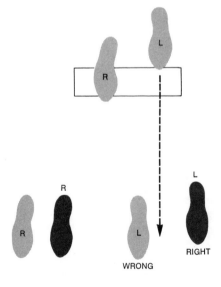

left foot has landed too soon, with the result that the arm and body movements are out of sync. Again, the body rhythm has been spent before the release, and the pitcher is just throwing with his arm. Also, in an unopened position the pitcher's weight will not be resting solely on his left foot but will be equally divided between his right foot and left foot. This forces his body to lunge to the right of the plate. The pitcher's arm, instead of crossing in front of his chest and down toward his left ankle, will shoot out straight, and the ball will travel high and inside without good speed. To find out if you are not opening up enough, merely remain in your follow-through for a second. If your weight is too heavily on your right foot and your arm finishes up alongside your right foot instead of your left, you definitely have not opened up enough.

Incorrect Follow-Through

The pitcher's arm has not crossed his chest and his weight is too centered. Result: a high, inside, weak pitch.

WEIGHT

Still another error of young pitchers is taking too short a stride. The stride should be as long as is comfortably possible while still permitting good balance. Too short a stride will cause the ball to be released early, resulting in a high pitch. Too long a stride will result in an exceptionally low pitch—which, however, is always better than a high one. A pitcher has only to adjust his stride a bit after each pitch to raise or lower his fastball. If he follows through too far to his left, the ball will be too far off the left-hand corner of the plate; too far to the right and the pitch will be too far off the right-hand corner. A simple adjustment in the follow-through should correct either problem.

A fourth common error made by young pitchers occurs when pushing off the rubber with the pivot foot. Sometimes, instead of letting the pivot foot follow through toward the batter, a young pitcher may either leave the foot anchored at the rubber or let it drag along the ground behind his body. In either case, his momentum will be slowed, which will result in a less than potent pitch. Remember, allow that pivot foot to swing high and forward until it lands alongside the other foot.

Falling Off the Mound

By not striding far enough, the pitcher lurches sideways and is in no position to field a ball batted back at him.

Former Cardinal great Bob Gibson was known for his awesome fastball, but look at his follow-through!

Some pitchers, like Bob Gibson, the former St. Louis Cardinal great, put so much effort into each pitch that they literally fall off the mound. The pivot foot, instead of falling parallel to the kicking foot, shoots far forward and to the left, so that the pitcher's back is to the batter. This makes it very difficult for the pitcher to field bunts or balls hit through the box (although in Gibson's case, his catlike reflexes more than made up for his errant follow-through), a price some are willing to pay for the extra momentum they get into each pitch. If a pitcher must err in his follow-through, this extreme delivery at least has the added bonus of producing a few more miles per hour on a fastball.

THE CLASSIC MOTION

Although Tom Seaver's pitching motion was as distinct from Jim Palmer's as Sandy Koufax's delivery was from Whitey Ford's, all great pitchers have a number of things in common. They all throw with a smooth, extended arm motion; they all drive off the rubber in a powerful manner with their pivot foot; and they all follow through toward the batter in a consistent way. Warren Spahn once proved to a young rookie in spring training that he could throw perfect strikes time after time with his eyes closed, because his arm followed the same trajectory on every pitch and his feet followed through into the same spot on every pitch. No matter how varied one great pitcher's motion is from another's, his own motion never varies from pitch to pitch. That is the secret to great control and to getting the maximum out of every delivery. Some, like Seaver, have a tight, muscular, drawing-in delivery that explodes toward the batter. Others, like Jim Palmer and Dwight Gooden, have an easy, almost effortless-looking delivery that makes them look as if they are merely playing a game of catch with their catcher. Others, like former pitching greats Juan Marichal and Warren Spahn, have a very stylized, meticulous delivery (exceptionally high kick and reach-back) that looks very deliberate, as if every pitch to them was a work of art. Still, no matter what form their delivery takes, each of these great pitchers goes through the different stages of a delivery with seldom a variance from pitch to pitch. On the following pages, our ideal pitcher executes each stage of his classic motion, without the artistic variations of many of the great pitchers we have talked about, but still in a classically perfect way that any young pitcher can emulate.

Many major-league pitchers today model their pitching motions after the stylized, high-kicking delivery of Warren Spahn, who pitched in the forties, fifties, and sixties for the Braves.

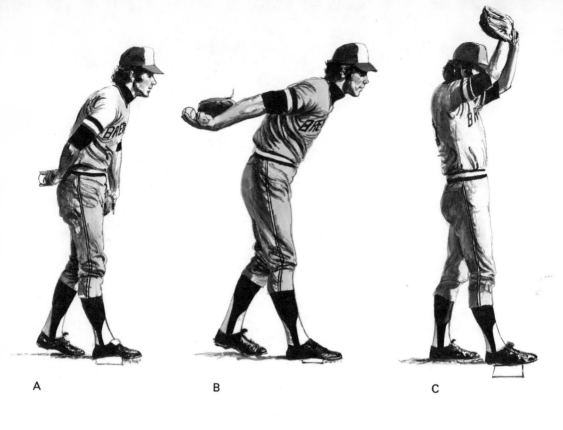

A
B
C

G
H

D   E   F

The Total Motion

It is all here: proper stance, kick, stride, release, and follow-through, each element essential to a proper motion. The all-important mechanics of the motion should be constantly practiced and refined.

I   J

THE STRETCH MOTION

With a runner on first base, the pitcher takes his sign standing sideways to the batter, his right foot already parallel to the rubber. His left foot should be about 8 inches in front of his right foot and a few inches to the left. His weight should rest mostly on his slightly flexed right leg, his left leg straight and supporting only a minimum of his weight. In fact, he is almost leaning back toward first base, as if he were going to wheel at any moment and try to pick

The Stretch: Foot Position

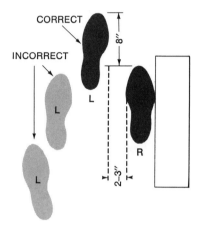

the runner off. Now, with his hands joined at his waist, the pitcher is ready to begin his motion. All he has to do is raise his left leg straight up and he will find himself in the perfect crane position (shown on page 21). This stretch motion allows him to get into the crane position very quickly, thus foiling a runner who is attempting to steal. The more motion a pitcher takes before he gets into the crane position, the more time a runner has to steal.

A common mistake of young pitchers is to take their sign in the stretch position but either with their left and right feet side by side or with the left foot behind the right foot. In this position, once the pitcher raises his left leg, he has to swing it toward third base before swinging it back toward the plate, losing valuable time, during which the runner can steal. Some pitchers claim that

The Stretch Position

Note how the pitcher's left foot is in front of his right. This allows him maximum efficiency when he raises his left leg into the crane position.

positioning their left foot more toward first base makes it easier for them to wheel and throw over to first. However, since a pitcher's primary concern is to hold a runner on the base, not to pick him off—a rare occurrence—he should use the stretch position diagramed on page 40. From this position he can deliver the ball to the plate more quickly than from any other position and can allow a runner the least time to take off.

The Pickoff, First Base

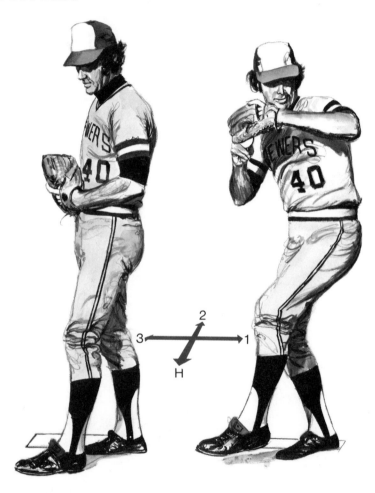

The pitcher pivots on his right foot, wheels his left foot around, and throws.

When a pitcher does throw to first, he simply pivots on his right foot 43

(touching the rubber) and wheels his left foot around from third base to first base. In attempting a pickoff at second base, he makes the same movements, only his left foot swings all the way around from third base, past home plate and first base to second base. It's almost as if he were performing a dancer's pirouette. In a pickoff attempt at third (which is identical to a left-handed

pitcher attempting to pick off a runner at first), the right-handed pitcher merely raises his left leg until he is in the crane position and then, instead of kicking toward third base and swinging his leg around toward home plate, kicks toward third base and throws straight to the bag. This is the easiest pickoff motion of all.

The Pickoff, Second Base

A   B

The pivot movement is like a dancer's pirouette.

The Pickoff, Third Base

C

The pitcher, in the stretch position, simply steps toward third base with his left foot and throws.

B

A

THE ARM MOTION

There are three basic arm motions: overhand, three-quarters overhand, and sidearm. A pitcher should throw with the motion most comfortable to him. He also should stick to one motion and not switch back and forth between, say, sidearm and overhand. True, some pitchers, like former Red Sox great Luis Tiant, are able to master a variety of arm motions, but they are the exception. If a pitcher throws every pitch—fastball, curveball, change-up—with the same motion, the batter will more easily be deceived. The ball will always come toward him at the same angle, yet it will be doing different things each time. This is the height of deception. The secret lies in the appearance of sameness and the reality of change.

The Overhand Motion

Most power pitchers, like Gooden and Roger Clemens, who rely mainly on explosive fastballs, throw with either a straight overhand or a three-quarters

The Overhand Fastball.
(A) As the pitcher's throwing arm moves past his head, his shoulders are tilted toward first and his arm is partly bent. (B) Rear view.

A

B

**Overhand Fastball:
Incorrect Positions.**
(A) The pitcher's arm is too straight, the elbow locked. Result: loss of power and speed. (B) The pitcher's arm is overly bent, which makes it difficult for him to apply shoulder power.

A

B

overhand motion. This motion allows the pitcher to get more of his upper body (upper back, shoulders) into each pitch. Assuming he is in the crane position, to throw the ball overhand the pitcher reaches back with his arm and down toward second base almost to the point of touching the ground. When his body and arm begin to move forward, the arm travels forward and up until it rises to a point 18 to 24 inches above and to the side of his right ear. His shoulders should be tilted so that his left shoulder is pointing down toward first base and his right shoulder is pointing up toward third base.

At this point the pitcher's arm is partially bent in a modified L design and not fully extended. If it is straight, he will lose the whiplike elbow action that gives his fastball much of its speed. His arm will be stiff, and he will be flinging the ball mostly with back and shoulder power. On the other hand, if his arm is bent too much at the elbow, he will be "slingshotting" the ball, as a catcher does, using mostly the strength of his forearm and losing much of the shoulder action that gives his fastball its speed.

Pushing

When the elbow gets ahead of the wrist, most shoulder power is lost, resulting in a weak, soft pitch.

Also at this point, the pitcher's arm from elbow to wrist should be vertical. If his elbow is ahead of his wrist, he will merely be pushing the ball toward the plate with his forearm, much in the same manner as an unathletic child throwing a ball. He will lose a lot of the important shoulder action.

Assuming that the pitcher's forearm is now vertical, the elbow even with his right ear, his arm continues its forward and downward motion toward the plate, but the moment the arm passes in front of his head, his wrist begins to move ahead of his elbow, and the arm begins to straighten out until the ball is released—about 15 inches in front of his head. At that point, the arm is almost but not quite straight. It straightens out completely only after the ball has left the hand. Also, at the moment of release, the pitcher's wrist snaps forward so that his wrist combines with his forearm, elbow, shoulders, and upper back to propel the ball forward and down. This wrist action puts a great

Approaching Release

As the pitcher's arm moves past his ear, his wrist is slightly ahead of his elbow.

deal of spin on the ball, giving a fastball most of the spinning motion which, cutting through the air currents, makes the ball move in one direction or another. A properly thrown overhand fastball will have an upward-spinning motion, causing the ball to rise.

After the hand has released the ball, the arm continues forward, down, and slightly to the left. It crosses the pitcher's chest and continues down until it comes to rest near the left ankle (as shown on page 29). If the arm only goes across the pitcher's chest and not down, he will lose the benefit of all the upper back motion which is propelling the rest of his body. This means that the arm motion will be going one way—right to left—while the body motion is going another—downward. Correct pitching requires that all the parts of the body move simultaneously in the same direction.

Besides generating maximum speed with this overhand motion, the pitcher

Wrist Snap

At the moment of release, the wrist snaps forward. This puts spin on a fastball and helps transmit the full power generated by the upper body.

also gains the advantage of delivering the ball at both a right-to-left and up-to-down angle. Thus the batter has to gauge not only the ball's speed but also the various angles of approach. And the more a batter must think before he can tell himself whether or not to swing, the more it is to the pitcher's advantage. The most difficult angle for a batter is an up-to-down one, rather than right-to-left. The obvious reason is that the bat is longer than it is wide. Because a bat is usually about 36 inches long and only about 4 inches wide—only 1 inch of which is true hitting wood—a hitter can more easily reach a right-to-left pitch than he can an up-to-down pitch. Of course, the ideal pitch moves in both directions, compounding the batter's computations.

The Three-Quarters Overhand Motion

The three-quarters overhand motion, used so successfully by Tom Seaver, is also an excellent motion for a fastball pitcher. When the pitcher is in his stride position, his arm will not be as high over his head with the three-quarters overhand motion as with the overhand delivery, nor will it be as close to his right ear. The elbow will be bent more, so that the arm is in a much tighter L shape than with the overhand motion. The pitcher's shoulders also are less tilted but are still not perfectly parallel to the ground. As the pitcher's arm moves forward and releases the ball, it will travel in more of a right-to-left direction than an up-to-down direction. This is the disadvantage of this motion as compared with a straight overhand delivery. However, the advantage is that it is easier to make a ball "move"—i.e., sink, rise, or tail in to a right-handed batter—with this motion than it is with an overhand delivery, which will generally cause the ball to move in only one direction—up—as it crosses the plate, and then only when a pitcher throws it with great speed. An overhand fastball without great speed is merely a straight pitch and is considerably easier to hit than a three-quarters fastball, which, though without great speed, has some additional movement on it as it crosses the plate. More on how to make pitches move in the next chapter, "The Pitches."

**Three-Quarters
Overhand Motion.**
The pitcher's shoulders are tilted less and his throwing arm bent more than in the overhand motion.

The Sidearm Motion

A sidearm pitch will generally have less speed than either a three-quarters or an overhand pitch, because the pitcher will lose much of his back and shoulder action and will be throwing the ball almost entirely with his arm. This pitch also puts a greater strain on a pitcher's arm, particularly his elbow, than either of the other pitches.

To throw a sidearm fastball, the pitcher starts in the crane position; then, when his throwing arm moves back, it rotates more toward first base—right to left—than back and down toward second, as with the other two motions. His whole arm and body motion is more right to left, with very little up and down. As the pitcher's arm moves toward the plate and passes alongside his head, the arm is almost perfectly parallel to the ground, with the ball at a level with his right ear. His shoulders also are parallel to the ground, with no up-down tilt. His elbow is only slightly bent. When his arm and body swing around from right to left toward the plate, there is practically no downward movement of

The Sidearm Motion.
The pitcher's arm is almost parallel to the ground and is slightly bent; his shoulders are level. Power is generated almost solely from the arm's whiplike rotational movement.

The pitch has a tendency to move in on a right-handed batter's hands.

his arm or body. The ball will approach the plate almost totally in a right-to-left direction, although there will be a slightly downward angle—the main disadvantage to this pitch. The advantages are that a sidearm pitch has a great deal of last-minute movement, especially tail and sink.

Even a major-league pitcher must tune up his motion from time to time.

Kent Tekulve throws sidearm almost exclusively. Since the sidearm delivery exerts strain on a pitcher's arm, Tekulve's success fluctuates greatly from year to year.

Most sidearm pitchers, like Kent Tekulve of the Phillies, have excellent sinkerballs, which makes them very good relievers, since sinkerballs are generally hit on the ground, helping to produce double plays.

As mentioned earlier, a pitcher should find that arm motion which feels most comfortable and then stick to it. What is comfortable to Kent Tekulve is not necessarily comfortable to Mike Scott or John Tudor. As E. B. White once said about writing, "The style is the man." You cannot go against your grain.

2

The Pitches ## THE FASTBALL

The pitch most thrown in major-league baseball and most often maligned is the fastball. "All big-league hitters murder fastballs" goes the consensus of professionals. A pitcher can't pitch successfully in the major leagues relying mainly on a fastball, yet more outs are recorded every game on the fastball than on any other single pitch. It is the basic pitch; every other pitch is a variation. Every pitcher, whether a knuckleball pitcher or a fastball pitcher, throws a fastball, yet not every pitcher throws a knuckleball, a slider, or even a curveball. Therefore, it is safe to say that the fastball is the most important pitch in any pitcher's arsenal. If he's basically a fastball pitcher, he needs that pitch for most of his outs and if he's a breaking-ball pitcher, he needs a fastball to offset his breaking balls. The irony is that most pitchers spend endless hours in the bullpen trying to improve their curveball, slider, and so forth, and generally neglect their fastball, feeling that the pitch is just a natural gift that they can't improve. Wrong! Even their natural limits can be extended. Any pitcher can learn to throw his fastball harder than he ever imagined he could, throw it to the right spot at an

59

One of today's great fastball pitchers, Roger Clemens.

appropriate moment, and finally, throw it so that it does not merely approach the plate in a straight line but at the last second takes an additional rise, dip, or tail.

Reflections on the Fastball

In the summer of 1960, I was a young, cocky minor-league pitcher who lived and died with his fastball. I remember one night I stepped out of the dugout to start a game against the hard-hitting White Sox of Clinton, Iowa, of the Class-D Midwest League. I overheard my fellow pitchers on the bench talking about the Sox's awesome hitter, Jim Hicks. You've gotta give him breaking stuff, they agreed. He kills fastballs. I looked over my shoulder and said, "He kills *your* fastballs, maybe, but he won't kill *my* fastball." That night I struck out Jim Hicks three times. I threw him nothing but fastballs down the middle of the plate. He swung through them all, with such force that he fell to one knee and had to right himself with his bat. There were times during that game when I knew I could fool him with a curveball, but I never threw him one. I just threw fastball after fastball, and he kept swinging as hard as he could, falling to one knee each time. The sight of him on one knee, righting himself like an old, defeated man after swinging through one of my fastballs was what I pitched for.

Despite an unsuccessful career (I never did make the major leagues—I lost my fastball along the way), I knew even then, as a 19-year-old pitcher, that a fastball, a good fastball, is the best pitch in baseball. I think, even today, it still is, which is why I was somewhat shocked a few seasons ago when I heard that Pete Rose had said fastball pitchers are a dying breed. Rose went on to say he just doesn't see that many good fastballs anymore. Whether he meant that today's pitchers don't throw as hard as pitchers of years gone by, or whether he simply meant that today's pitchers don't throw as many fastballs as pitchers once did, was not explained.

A great fastball like Koufax's or Nolan Ryan's or Bob Feller's is a gift that can never be learned, but any fastball, no matter how modest, can be improved upon with proper coaching. Therefore, to varying degrees, every pitcher's fastball is a gift. Where does this gift reside? Some pitchers, like Seaver, think it comes from the legs—and the ability to drive off the mound with force—as much as from the upper arm and shoulder (which is why a leg injury is so damaging to a fastball pitcher, while an arm injury may be only bothersome).

Seaver was a skinny youth in high school and, as such, had only a modest fastball. He claimed that only as he developed physically—gained muscle and size through his legs, chest, and shoulders—did his fastball begin to pop. He was a classic "grunter," a fastball pitcher like Goose Gossage or Roger Clemens who relies on the sheer physical exertion of almost every part of his body for the speed of his fastball. Others, like Dwight Gooden, seem to throw the ball without effort, and still it pops. Why? Former Yankee pitching coach Sammy Ellis says it has to do with the nature of these pitchers' forearms. "Guys like [Ron] Guidry and Dave Righetti who seem to throw without effort," says Ellis, "get their speed from their forearm to their wrist. It's a God-given gift. You could nail their feet to the ground and they could still throw the ball ninety miles an hour just flipping it using their lower arm."

One of the fastest pitchers who ever lived, perennial minor leaguer Steve Dalkowski, who pitched in the Orioles' chain during the late fifties and early sixties, was reputed to be able to bend his wrist backward so that it touched his forearm. Dalkowski, who was also supposed to be able to throw a baseball well over 100 miles per hour (but rarely near the plate, which is why he never reached the majors), was taken to Johns Hopkins Hospital in Baltimore one year and tested by a host of physicians, none of whom could ever explain why such a slight man, built like Guidry, could throw a baseball so hard.

What all fastball pitchers, from "grunters" like Seaver, Clemens, and Gossage to effortless throwers like Guidry, Gooden, and Palmer, have in common, though, is a well-developed pitching motion that makes the most of their body types. Thin, long-armed pitchers generally have a loose, flowing motion that relies mostly on arm speed and wrist snap for their speed. Beefier pitchers rely more on the sheer physical exertion of every part of their body for their speed. A common fault of both types of pitchers, when their fastball is subpar, is their failure to synchronize their arm speed with their body's forward momentum. As discussed in Chapter 1, this is called "rushing," and it simply means that a pitcher's body is moving too quickly, that it is out of sync with his arm. While the body is planted firmly in the follow-through, the arm is still trailing behind, which usually results in an ineffectual high fastball, thrown solely with the arm and without using any of the body's already spent momentum. Rushing usually comes from a pitcher's lack of patience. Young pitchers can't wait to deliver the ball, and neither can more emotional types; the result in both cases is a too-quick delivery that leaves the arm trailing behind.

"I get so wrapped up in situations," says Gossage, "the excitement of the game, that I can't wait to get the ball and throw it again. It's my worst habit. My body gets out in front of my arm. People don't realize how hard you have

Rich Gossage is a classic example of the "grunter": the pitcher who puts everything he has behind his fastball—and shows it.

to work at a fastball. They think it just comes. One year early in my career, I was working a lot on my breaking ball, and neglecting my fastball. I just thought it would always be there. I didn't realize you have to work on it as much as any other pitch. I still am."

When a fastball pitcher is throwing at his best, he seems to be throwing effortlessly. This is no illusion. There seems to be an almost mythical groove all fastball pitchers search for, a place where their arm motion and leg motion flow perfectly, as if in a vacuum, without resistance—and when they find it, whether for a game, or an inning, or just a pitch, they are unhittable.

"When I'm throwing right," says Dave Righetti, "it all seems effortless. That happens maybe five or six times a year. A young pitcher has to accept that or else he spends all his time searching for that great fastball, always trying to force it when he shouldn't. You need patience."

Despite the obvious advantages of having a good fastball, most pitchers would agree that the pitch has more than its share of drawbacks. It's a hard pitch to control because it requires such a delicate balance of proper pitching mechanics in a way that breaking balls don't. Furthermore, a fastball is highly susceptible to the onslaughts of age and injury. Even a slight arm injury, or merely advancing years, will diminish a pitcher's fastball just enough to make it hittable. As Sammy Ellis says, "A ninety-six-mile-an-hour fastball is an 'out' pitch; a ninety-three-mile-an-hour fastball is good hitting speed." (It is ironic that pitchers with great fastballs do not put more stress on their arms than pitchers with only modest fastballs. Both types are throwing as hard as they can and are putting the maximum stress on their arms, despite the differences in the speed of their fastballs. It is also ironic that when a pitcher with a modest fastball either hurts his arm or grows old and loses a few miles per hour off his pitch, the result is not as devastating as when a pitcher with a superior fastball suffers the same consequences.)

One final drawback of all fastball pitchers is that they have to work harder than breaking-ball pitchers, because batters miss their pitches more often. Batters swing through perfect strikes or foul them off time after time, whereas with a breaking-ball pitcher they might hit the first pitch routinely to second base. Fastball pitchers seldom get "easy" outs. Often, they have to throw twice as many pitches in a game to produce the same results. One rarely sees a fastball pitcher ring up the kind of 98-pitch game that a Bert Blyleven or a Fernando Valenzuela will.

Today, most baseball people think that the game's present-day pitchers don't throw as hard as pitchers of twenty, thirty, or forty years ago. The reasons are myriad. Don Zimmer, the former Yankee coach and Red Sox manager, claims this is so because of the advent of the slider in the early sixties. "You didn't see sliders before that," says Zimmer. "Today, a kid with a good fastball can master a great slider easily. Pretty soon he's throwing so many sliders it takes away from his fastball." Ron Guidry might be a perfect example of such a pitcher. Despite a decent fastball in his prime, Guidry has always considered himself predominantly a slider-ball pitcher. A slider, which is either a quick, sharp curveball or a fastball that breaks, depending on your viewpoint, is a devastating pitch when thrown at 90-plus miles per hour. More devastating, in fact, than a 95-mile-per-hour fastball. However, it puts a great strain on a pitcher's arm, and after a few years, most pitchers will have lost their good fastball.

"I think pitchers had better arms years ago," says Jim Palmer. "Today they learn to throw breaking balls at an early age and never give their fastball time to develop when they're young. They seem to be in a hurry to reach the majors, and think breaking balls will get them there. Gene Woodling once told me that the toughest pitch to hit is a good fastball. You can make a mistake with it and the batter will pop it up."

Joe Torre, the former Braves' manager and a former catcher behind Bob Gibson, one of the hardest throwing pitchers ever, agrees with Palmer. He says, "I don't think young pitchers throw enough fastballs today. It's the best pitch in baseball. They're too anxious to be too cute too soon in their careers. They say hitters murder good fastballs, but that's not true. They murder *bad* fastballs." Torre goes on to relate a story about two minor-league pitchers he worked behind in the early sixties when he was a catcher in the Braves' chain. One was Larry Maxie, the other Tony Cloninger. Both were hard-throwing bonus babies who began their careers in the low minors with different degrees of success. Maxie, throwing mainly fastballs, had an exceptional minor-league career until he reached the Triple-A level, where he began experimenting with off-speed and breaking-ball pitches, because he believed the old axiom that major-league hitters murder good fastballs. Cloninger, who at one time in Class-D ball was 0–9, had an indifferent minor-league career with his fastball. But he never despaired of it, and eventually it propelled him into the major leagues, where he had some excellent seasons, including a 24-victory season with the Braves. Maxie never did make the majors, after having lost his fastball, which he could never recapture.

"A lot of young fastball pitchers abandon their pitch because of a fear of failure," says retired fastballer Jon Matlack. "They want to be perfect today. They don't want to see that good fastball rocked for a home run and have to come back with it again. There's always an excuse if they hit your curveball: 'It hung.' 'It didn't break.' You know. But guys like Catfish Hunter, they weren't afraid to get hurt with their fastball and come back right at you with it. That takes guts. You have to stay within your limits, no matter what. You can't panic and abandon your best pitch."

Jim Hegan, an ex-Yankee coach, was once a catcher with the Cleveland Indians and worked behind the plate with Early Wynn, Bob Lemon, Mike

Garcia, and Bob Feller, some of the hardest throwing pitchers in the history of the game. Sitting in the Yankees' locker room one day, Hegan looked down to the end of the bench at the current crop of Yankee pitchers, and said, "I see these kids, they're bigger, stronger, and throw harder than most of the pitchers, except for Feller, that I saw in my time." Bob Lemon, one-time battery mate of Hegan's and later manager of the Yankees, agrees. Lemon claims that the major difference between fastball pitchers today and in his day, is that they talk more about their breaking pitches. Today, the slider and the split-fingered fastball are the "in" pitches in baseball, in a way that the overpowering fastball was the "in" pitch twenty years ago and earlier. Today's fastball pitcher would rather talk, say, about his slider, because it is a learned pitch. He can take credit for it, whereas his fastball was merely a gift he thinks he has had little to do with.

Wayne Terwilliger, a nine-year major-league player during the fifties who became a Texas Ranger coach, says that when he played pitchers threw him four fastballs out of every five pitches, but now young pitchers rarely throw so many fastballs to a batter, no matter how good their fastball is. "I think they have a different philosophy today," says Terwilliger. "They don't think they can get by with a good fastball, even when they have it." Terwilliger points out that in a recent newspaper story Dave Righetti, possessor of one of the best fastballs in the game, was quoted as saying he can't win with his fastball unless he can get his breaking stuff over the plate as well. Yet, in the fifties and before, pitchers like Robin Roberts, a perennial twenty-game winner with the Phillies, got by year after year proudly admitting they had no curveball, only a fastball.

"I faced Roberts," says Terwilliger, "and I don't think he threw anywhere near as hard as some of these kids do today. He just thought he did."

The point Terwilliger is making is that years ago pitchers had more confidence in their fastballs even when they weren't truly exceptional. In the twilight of his career, Robin Roberts had only a faint hint of his former fastball, but still he considered himself a fastball pitcher. Before starting a game shortly before he retired, he told a young pitcher on his team, "Watch, I'll still get 'em out with my fastball," and he did, much to the young pitcher's amazement. That pitcher, Bill Hands, himself eventually a 20-game winner in the major leagues, said, "I couldn't believe it. He had nothing, and there he was throwing fastballs up and in like it was a hundred-mile-an-hour pitch, and I'll be damned if he didn't get 'em out."

There have been only a few pitchers like that in the major leagues in recent years. Jim Palmer was one. Even in the later years of his career he still threw

In contrást to Gossage's delivery, Jim Palmer's looked effortless. Still, he always threw a mean fastball.

his fastball up and in to batters—supposedly a dangerous pitch scorned by younger, harder-throwing pitchers—yet he did so successfully. When Tom Seaver posted a 14–2 record in the strike-shortened season of 1981, he was telling everyone who would listen that he had lost a lot off his fastball and had had to change his pitching style—throw more change-ups and breaking balls, try to make his fastball sink. After his comments were duly recorded in the press, Seaver would tell a friend, with a wink, "Sure, I lost a little off my fastball, but I can still bring it ninety-four miles an hour when I have to. But I don't want anyone to know that. I want them to think I lost it. So I throw a few more change-ups in a game, let the batters think I don't have that good fastball anymore, and then bust it in on them." He laughed. He was still the same type of pitcher he always was.

Today pitchers like Seaver and Palmer are becoming rare. It is as if younger pitchers have talked themselves out of relying on their best pitch, or maybe the hitters, shrewdly, have talked the pitchers out of it, just as those minor leaguers tried to talk me out of it years ago when I faced Jim Hicks. "Jim Hicks murders fastballs," they said. I didn't listen then, and you shouldn't listen now. No one murders Sandy Koufax's fastball, or Roger Clemens', or Goose Gossage's (well, in Gossage's case, no one except maybe George Brett). If you stick to the following advice, you won't be guaranteed a Sandy Koufax fastball, but you will be assured that you can improve that basic pitch to the point where batters will start telling you not to throw it anymore because everyone knows they murder fastballs.

The Fastball Grip

There is only one basic way to grip the ball, regardless of whether a pitcher throws his fastball with an overhand, three-quarters, or sidearm motion. It is gripped with the first two fingers of the hand cutting directly across the center of the ball. Those fingers should be close together, not spread apart. The pressure points on the ball should be the center, meaty part of those two fingertips, not the extreme tips. The ball should not be gripped tightly, jammed against the inside of the pitcher's hand, but should be held with a slight air space between the ball and the hand. The thumb grips the underside of the ball as another pressure point, but the extreme tip of the thumb should not press on the ball; the pressure should be on that meaty part of the thumb closer to the knuckle. The third pressure point is located on the side of the ball where the pitcher's third finger is knuckled under. The pressure is directly against the knuckle of that third finger. To repeat, the ball should not be jammed tightly into the pitcher's hand, but should be held with a slight air space between the ball and the inner palm. Also, the fingers should not be wrapped tightly around the ball, merely firmly. The only tight pressure on the ball should be at the three pressure points. It is this pressure which gives the fastball its excessive spinning motion at the point of release. A ball held tightly all over will not spin as much as one held tightly only at the pressure points.

The Fastball Grip

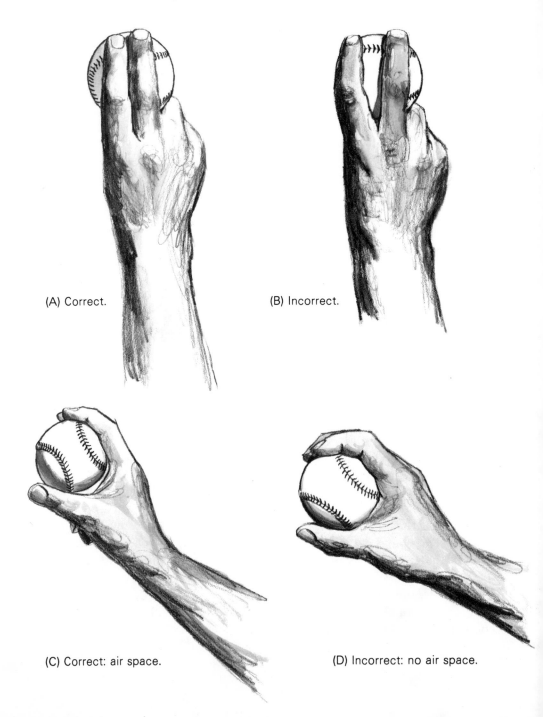

(A) Correct.

(B) Incorrect.

(C) Correct: air space.

(D) Incorrect: no air space.

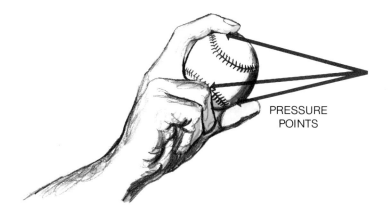

PRESSURE
POINTS

The basic fastball is held with the first two fingers bisecting the ball's seams on top and the thumb bisecting the seam on the bottom. The pressure points in both places are directly on the seams, which operate almost like handles to give the pitcher a firm grip on the ball. When the pitch is thrown, the pitcher's

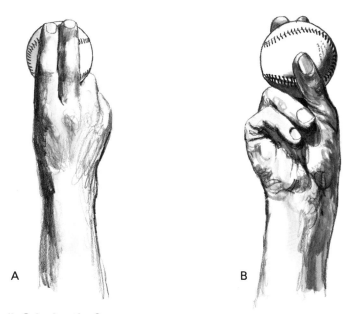

A

B

The Fastball: Gripping the Seams.
The pressure points are on the seams: the first two fingers cross the top seam (A); the thumb bisects the bottom seam (B).

Fastball Spin

Upward spin is put on a fast-ball when the two top fingers pull down and across the top seam and the thumb pushes forward.

top two fingers pull down on the top seam, directly cutting through the heart of the ball and causing the ball to spin upward. At the same moment, the pitcher's thumb is pushing forward on the other seam, which accelerates the spin. This double action against the seams produces an upward spin at maximum speed and makes the ball look smaller as it approaches the batter—an optical illusion that serves to the pitcher's advantage. A slower-spinning ball looks large and easy to hit, with its red seams more visible to the batter, whereas a fast-spinning ball becomes merely a small white blur with no sharply defined edges or seams. The fast spinning also has the advantage of giving the ball a certain last-second movement as it reaches the plate.

An overhand fastball should cross the plate with a rising motion. A three-quarters fastball should be spinning up and slightly off center, crossing the plate both rising and tailing in to a right-handed hitter. And a sidearm fastball should be spinning directly parallel to the ground.

Some pitchers try to make their fastballs "move" by artificial means. They deliberately cut through the ball off center so that the ball will spin off center and move in a desired direction. For example, when a pitcher throwing over-

The Three-Quarters Fastball

The three-quarters fastball spins slightly off center, causing it to rise and tail in to a right-handed batter.

The Sidearm Fastball

The sidearm fastball spins parallel to the plate, which causes it to tail in or sink as it crosses the plate.

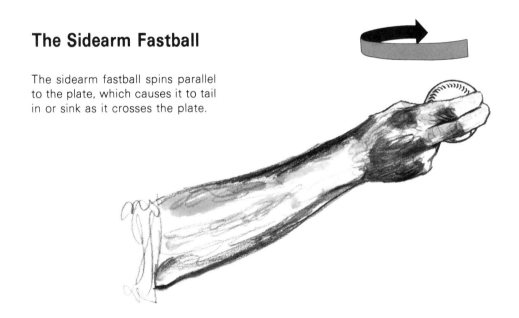

Different Fastballs:
A Right-Handed Batter's View

An overhand fastball rises as it crosses the plate (A); a three-quarters fastball rises and tails in (B).

Making a Fastball Move

Both three-quarters and overhand pitchers make their fastballs move by rolling their fingers to the left as they release the ball.

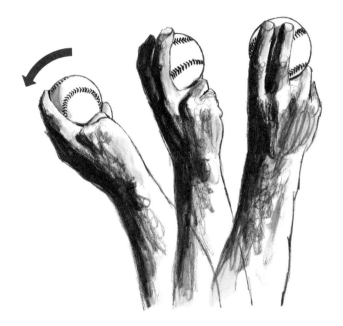

hand or three-quarters tries to make a ball move artificially, he will cut down through and slightly to the left of the ball, with his first two fingers rolling off the ball to the left. This motion generally makes the fastball tail or rise or both. A sidearm pitcher will cut through and over the top of the ball to make it sink. These "artificially" thrown fastballs, also called "sinkerballs," have the advantage of more movement than a regularly thrown fastball, but a pitcher loses speed when he no longer cuts directly through the heart of the ball.

Most fastballs should be thrown in one of two spots: low and away from a batter, or high and inside. These are the two most difficult fastballs for a batter to hit. To hit a low-and-outside fastball, a batter must reach both out and down for the pitch, which, if thrown fast enough, will already be past him. He has only to reach directly outside for a high-outside fastball, which makes it a much easier pitch to hit. The advantage of a high-and-inside fastball is that the closer the pitch gets to a batter's eye, the greater its speed appears to be. It is an optical

The Moving Sidearm Fastball

To make a sidearm fastball move, cut through and over the ball as you release it (A).

The ball should either tail in (B), or sink (C).

Famed sidearm reliever Dan Quisenberry throwing his bread-and-butter pitch. Note the position of his throwing hand, which has just cut through and over the ball as he released it.

illusion, really, but one which invariably throws off a batter's timing. So, these are the ideal spots, and a pitcher should work back and forth between them in setting up a batter.

Whether the fastball goes low and away or up and in is determined by the point at which the ball leaves the pitcher's hand. A right-handed pitcher throwing to a right-handed batter can make the ball go up and in by releasing

Spotting the Fastball

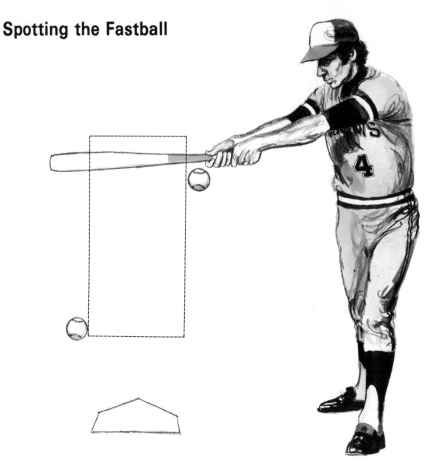

High and inside or low and away is the pitcher's best target for the fastball.

the ball soon after it passes his ear. To make the fastball travel low and on the outside corner of the plate, the pitcher merely holds onto the ball longer and releases it farther out in front of his head. Knowing when to release the ball is a question of "feel." Feel is not easy to come by and takes a great deal of practice, which is why control is such an elusive element for most pitchers. However, if a pitcher throws with a classically correct motion, his chances for acquiring a high degree of feel are excellent.

A pitcher uses different release points to move his fastball. An early release (A) produces a high, inside pitch to a right-handed batter; a normal release (B) puts the ball across the center of the plate; a slightly delayed release (C) puts the ball down and outside.

THE CURVEBALL

The curveball is the favorite pitch of every young pitcher. He approaches it with wonder. Imagine! The ability to make a thrown ball change directions on the way to the plate! Youngsters can't wait to throw their first curveball, but often this will hinder their future career for a number of reasons. A curveball is the most difficult pitch to throw properly. It requires years of practice beginning only after a pitcher has perfected the control and delivery of his fastball. Otherwise, he is wasting his time even trying to learn the pitch. Some pitchers, like Tom Seaver, never learn to control it properly, while to

Master of the curveball: Bert Blyleven.

others, like Bert Blyleven, it comes so easily that it eventually becomes their bread-and-butter pitch.

If not properly thrown, a curveball will cause an injury to a young pitcher's arm. Therefore, it is necessary for young pitchers to strengthen their arms first before even beginning to try to master this difficult pitch. Even if they do master it at a young age, it will have a deteriorating effect on their careers. Too many curveballs thrown too soon in a young pitcher's career will weaken his arm and prevent him from ever developing that good fastball he will need in order to succeed. A pitcher strengthens his arm by putting strain on it—by throwing hard—and the effortless motion of a properly thrown curveball puts very little strain on a young pitcher's arm. Thus, his fastball never develops. Furthermore, whenever young pitchers acquire a good curveball early in their careers, they tend to rely on it too much. Bert Blyleven, for example, has always had one of the greatest curveballs in the game, and yet he has only occasionally been better than a .500 pitcher with a variety of clubs. Why? Some critics say it's because he relied too heavily on his curveball, and his excellent fastball suffered. (Of course, it may also be because, except for the Minnesota Twins, Blyleven has not played for many teams that scored a lot of runs for him!) Tom Seaver, on the other hand, devoted his career to mastering every aspect of his craft because he could never come up with that great curveball that would make pitching too easy for him. The result: a Hall of Fame pitcher.

Another drawback to throwing curveballs is that the pitch must either be thrown perfectly or not at all. A curveball is either right on the money or an easy pitch to hit. There are no in-betweens with it. Properly thrown, it should end up low and off the outside of the plate when thrown by a right-handed pitcher to a right-handed batter, and low and inside when thrown by a right-hander to a left-handed batter. A hanging curveball—one thrown waist high over the middle of the plate or even higher—is a sucker pitch. It seems that after every game a pitcher can be found talking about the home run that beat him which was hit off a "hanging curveball" that got away from him.

A truly great, sharp-breaking curveball is not only difficult to hit but also difficult to catch and to judge in relation to the strike zone. More than one curveball thrown for a strike has handcuffed a catcher, allowing a runner on first to steal second. And more than one veteran umpire has called a curveball thrown for a perfect strike a ball because he couldn't judge its progress. The difficulty in calling a curveball lies in the fact that it must be called where it crosses the plate, not where the catcher catches it. Some great curveballs look as if they are in the dirt when they arrive at the catcher, yet they crossed the plate at the level of the batter's knee. Others arrive at the catcher knee-high in the middle of the plate, yet when they passed the plate they were high to the batter.

If a curveball has so many drawbacks, then why bother to throw it? The answer is easy. When perfected, it is the second best pitch in baseball and will help make the first best pitch, a fastball, even more powerful. In the minors, one of my managers referred to a great curveball as "the unfair one." When perfect, it is almost unhittable. Every great strikeout pitcher, no matter how hard he throws (Nolan Ryan, Dwight Gooden), gets at least half of his strike-outs with his curveball.

When properly thrown, a curveball puts very little strain on a pitcher's arm. It requires a more natural movement of the arm than a fastball. A pitcher's arm shoots forward at a great strain when throwing a fastball, but it actually makes a big, soft, sweeping circle when throwing a curveball.

Precisely because a curveball is thrown at a lesser speed than a fastball is what makes it such a helpful pitch. It is a great change-of-pace off an explosive fastball, no matter how insignificant or how sharply it breaks. A curveball is best used to supplement a fastball. It is a No. 2 pitch. It was never meant to supplant a fastball. Now, let's learn how to throw one.

The best-breaking curveball is the one which breaks straight down, with little or no right-to-left break. This seems to contradict an earlier statement that a ball moving in two directions—down *and* right to left—is preferable to a ball moving in only one direction. However, this rule does not apply to a curveball, since, if it is thrown properly, it will spin like a fastball, only in the opposite direction—downward. Approaching the batter, a down-breaking curveball appears to be spinning like a fastball, and the batter, looking down on it, is unable to tell when the ball begins to break. His vantage point—looking down on a sinking object—creates an optical illusion. However, if that same curveball were also breaking from right to left, the batter could pick up that point at which the ball begins to break from right to left, tell himself the pitch was a curveball, and adjust his swing accordingly. Another reason it is easier to hit a right-to-left breaking curveball than a straight-down-breaking one is that a batter has almost 36 inches of bat length with which to reach the one breaking horizontally, while he has only about 1 inch of bat width to hit the one that is breaking straight down. Also, the down-breaking curveball is equally effective whether thrown to a right-handed or a left-handed batter.

But whatever kind of curveball, the grip remains the same. The pitcher's first two fingers are tight together but running parallel to the ball's seams, not

The Curveball Grip

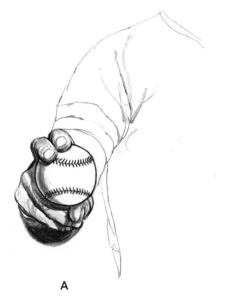

(A) The ball is gripped tighter and deeper in the hand than it is with the fastball. Notice that the fingers are parallel to and gripping the seams.

(B) Thumb pressure is applied against the seam.

A   B

bisecting them, as with the fastball. The second finger rides alongside the seam, and the first finger presses against the second finger. The pressure points run all along the length of the fingers rather than only at the meaty tips, as with a fastball. The thumb runs parallel to the seam on the underside of the ball and exerts pressure against it all along the length of the thumb and not just at the knuckle. And the ball is gripped much tighter than a fastball, with almost no air space between the inside of the palm and the ball. The knuckle of the third finger is also pressed against a seam, so that when the pitcher releases the ball he actually has three sustained pressure points on the seams to give the ball a maximum amount of spin.

To throw a straight down-breaking curveball, a pitcher must throw the ball with an overhand motion. However, until his arm passes alongside his head, he does nothing different from when he is throwing a fastball: his first two fingers on the baseball are still aimed directly at the plate. Only when the ball passes in front of his head do changes take place which turn an apparent fastball into a curveball. His first two fingers begin to ride up and over the ball

The Curveball: Arm Motion

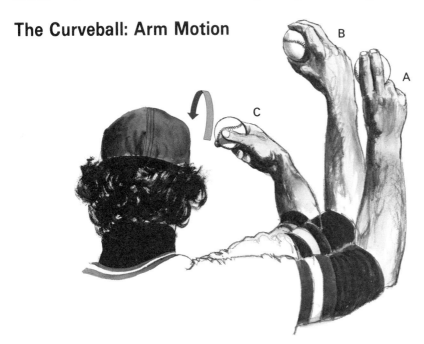

The first two fingers ride up and over the ball (A) while the arm moves from right to left and downward in a kind of yanking motion (B). The wrist bends forward at the release (C), so that the ball rolls off the two forward fingers.

The Curveball: Full Motion

(A) Until the throwing arm moves past the head, the pitching motion is the same as for the fastball.

(B) Only as the arm continues forward does the yanking motion begin with the fingers giving the ball its downward spin.

while simultaneously turning from right to left. Just before the ball passes above and in front of his vision, he yanks his first two fingers down over the side of the ball facing the batter. His wrist continues to rotate forward and down, and his forearm is yanked sharply from right to left and down. When the ball is in front of his vision and at a level with his cap (his forearm is now bent almost parallel to his vision), his first two fingers should be facing the batter and his thumb facing his vision. At this point the ball spins off his first two fingers, aided by a forward upthrusting motion of his thumb, and heads toward the plate with a severe down-spinning motion. His forearm continues passing down across his

(C) During the follow-through
the arm continues down and
across the body.

(D) The arm ends up wrapped
around the waist.

chest and in toward his left side, following through with his right hand tucked
in to the left of his waist, almost as if the arm were wrapped around a partner's
waist while dancing. This sharp yanking motion of both the wrist and the
forearm gives the ball its excessive downspin, which causes it to approach the
plate and suddenly drop sharply. To give the pitch its sharpest break, the
yanking motion should occur at a point about 6 inches in front of and above
the pitcher's vision. If a pitcher yanks too soon, the ball will have a larger, more
leisurely break, and will just roll up to the plate. This rolling type of curveball
is an excellent change-of-pace pitch, but it should not be a bread-and-butter

84

curveball. The sooner the pitcher cocks his wrist before reaching the release point, the slower and bigger will be the pitch's break.

If the pitcher finds himself breaking the curveball into the dirt instead of over the plate, the chances are he is not taking a long enough stride. His left foot is coming down too soon, causing him to yank and release early so that the ball breaks before it crosses the plate. To remedy this, a pitcher should merely lengthen his stride. Conversely, if the pitch is breaking too high as it crosses the plate, the pitcher's stride is probably too long and he should shorten it by bringing his left foot down sooner.

Ideally, all curveballs should break in one general area: over the lower outside corner of the plate. And the ideal curveball should break across the plate as a low strike caught by the catcher almost in the dirt. This pitch is almost impossible for a batter to hit solidly.

Both a three-quarters curveball and a sidearm curveball are thrown exactly the same way as the overhand curveball. However, because the angle of

The Curveball: Wrong Rotation

If the pitcher's hand comes around the ball instead of over it, his curve will fail to break, giving the batter an easy pitch to hit.

the arm in both cases is moving more right to left than straight down, the ball will have more of a right-to-left break. But it should also break down more sharply from a three-quarters angle than from a sidearm angle.

A common mistake all pitchers make occurs when the pitcher's fingers and wrist rotate from right to left around the ball rather than up and over the ball. This produces a flat curveball which has no downward break at all but which merely moves from right to left. Sometimes this curveball will even rise slightly into the batter's vision, making it the easiest of curveballs to hit.

THE SLIDER

The slider is a pitch about which many baseball people are ambivalent. On the one hand, it has made many an average pitcher into a great pitcher (witness former A's and Yankee great Catfish Hunter); on the other, it has diminished the long-range effectiveness of most fastballs to an extent no other pitch has. The slider has taken more out of the arms of hard-throwing pitchers (Ron Guidry, for example) than has any other pitch. It is a pitch most pitchers should turn to only when they have been presented with overwhelming evidence that their fastballs and curveballs are no longer adequate to get batters out. At best, Catfish Hunter had only a fair major-league fastball and his curveball was virtually nonexistent. The slider was the perfect pitch for Hunter to acquire. Yet Guidry, with his explosive fastball, began to rely heavily on his slider so early in his career that his fastball deteriorated much more rapidly than it would have if he had spent the time developing a good curveball to go with his fastball. It made Guidry a *great* pitcher one year (1978, when he was 25–3) and only a very good pitcher thereafter. Pitchers like Guidry turn quickly to the slider because it is so much easier to master than a good curveball. It's a shortcut to success that has its price. If Sandy Koufax had abandoned his great fastball and equally great curveball early in his career in favor of the slider, he might never have had the kind of overpowering years he had. Yet great pitchers, like Hunter, and lesser pitchers, like reliever Sparky Lyle, might never even have had major-league careers if they had not picked up the slider. Again: *A slider should be acquired only when a pitcher discovers his fastball and curveball will never be adequate by themselves to insure success as he progresses up the baseball ladder.*

Although a slider is one of the easiest pitches to learn to throw, it is also

The Slider: Batter's View

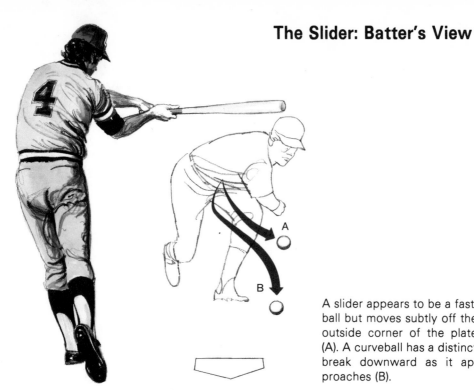

A slider appears to be a fast-ball but moves subtly off the outside corner of the plate (A). A curveball has a distinct break downward as it approaches (B).

The Slider Grip

A slider is gripped like a curveball but deeper in the hand and slightly off center.

one of the most difficult to control, since it must be thrown only to certain spots
or be exceedingly easy to hit. Pinpoint control is essential. Also, since a slider is a slip pitch thrown with a stiff wrist and a sharp snap of the elbow, it often produces a sore arm. Therefore, a pitcher working on a slider should quit the moment he feels any pain or stiffness in his elbow. A properly thrown curveball and fastball are nowhere nearly as dangerous to the arm as a slider.

Now to the advantages of a slider. It is an easy pitch, learned in minutes. It is extremely deceptive because it comes in hard; it appears to be a fastball; and at no point can one tell that it is a breaking pitch. Actually it does not break; it is more of a moving fastball than a curveball. A curveball can be graphed; that is, one can plot that point in its travel to the plate at which it begins to break. No such point can be plotted with a properly thrown slider. It appears to be heading for the center of the plate, but then, in the midst of his swing, the batter discovers that his calculations were off and that the ball has moved subtly and deceptively off the outside corner of the plate. A slider is ideally thrown when a batter is guessing fastball. As the ball approaches the heart of the plate, looking for all the world like a mediocre fastball, the batter will attack it and will probably either swing wildly or hit a routine fly ball or ground ball.

A slider is gripped like a curveball, only the ball is held deeper in the palm and slightly off center, so that more of the white of the ball is exposed between the first finger and thumb. A slider has already become a slider when the pitcher's hand passes alongside his head. Unlike a fastball or a curveball, both of which pass the pitcher's head with the first two fingers aiming at the plate, a slider passes the pitcher's head with the first two fingers slightly on top of the ball and aiming toward the outside corner of the plate. The pitcher's wrist is firmly cocked, almost as if he were throwing a football. As his arm follows through, at no point does his wrist rotate, as it does with a curveball, or flick forward and down, as it does with a fastball. His wrist must remain perfectly stiff so that his arm continues straight toward the plate with the ball held off center. At the moment of release the ball merely slips out of the pitcher's hand with an off-center, right-to-left, and downward spin. It approaches the plate moving slightly right to left and down, but at no point does it actually begin to break.

As mentioned before, a slider is an easy pitch to learn to throw, yet is a difficult pitch to control because it must be thrown almost entirely in one spot—low and on the outside corner of the plate to a right-handed batter and waist-high and inside to a left-handed batter. (The reverse is true for a left-handed pitcher.) A slider is the only breaking pitch occasionally thrown waist high—but only to an opposite-handed batter. An inside waist-high slider from a

Different Breaking Balls

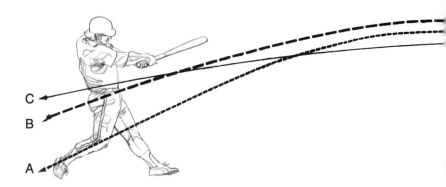

A curveball spins away from the pitcher, causing the ball to "break" sharply downward and cross below the batter's knees (A). A slow, "hanging" curve (B) fails to break sharply and has a gentle arc, usually because of the pitcher has yanked the ball too soon. A slider (C) appears not to break at all—an illusion: it actually breaks much later and more subtly than a curveball.

The Slider: Arm Motion

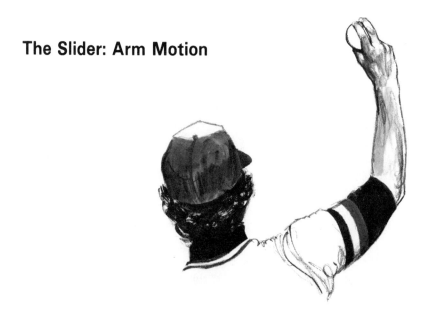

The pitcher's wrist is cocked and the fingers are slightly on top of the ball as the arm moves past the head (A).

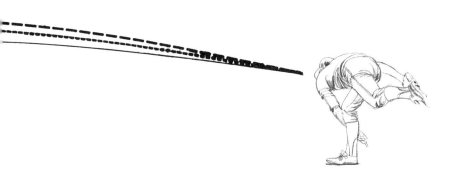

The wrist must remain stiff as the arm continues its forward movement (B).

At release (C), the ball rolls off the hand with an off-center spin. The wrist never breaks.

right-handed pitcher to a left-handed batter will be hit on the handle of the bat. If the pitch is thrown low and inside, the left-handed batter still has a chance to golf it down the right-field line.

THE CHANGE-UP

Stu Miller, a successful relief pitcher for the San Francisco Giants and the Baltimore Orioles during the sixties, threw so many change-ups during a typical game that it was said, derogatorily, that he simply placed the ball in the crook of his throwing arm and let his pulse carry it to the plate. The feeling was that there was something unmanly about retiring major-league batters with a pitch that was less than your best (i.e., hardest). It was like finding lost money: no credit to your initiative. The pitches that were the best were the ones you had to work hardest to throw.

Today, that kind of thinking no longer prevails in the major leagues. In fact, one of the pitchers who is most successful, and most feared and respected by batters, is Scott McGregor, of the Orioles, who makes his living throwing change-ups 80 percent of the time. In fact, when Scott tried to forge a big-league

The Change-Up

The change-up motion begins like a fastball's (A), but when the arm moves past the head, the elbow shoots ahead of the wrist and drops (B).

A   B

career as a conventional fastball-curveball pitcher, he failed. When he tried to develop a slider, he came up with a sore arm. It was only when he mastered a change-up that he developed into one of the best pitchers in the game. His former catcher, Rick Dempsey, once referred to Scott as "the master of the dead fish." That's what it's like for batters trying to hit his change-up, Dempsey said; the bat meeting the ball makes a splatting sound, and the ball seems to die off the bat on its way toward the outfield.

If the change-up is such a devastating pitch, if it puts virtually no strain on a pitcher's arm, why, then, do so few pitchers rely on it? The answer is simple. The change-up is one of the most difficult pitches to learn to throw and to control, despite the fact that throwing it looks so easy. It involves a play of opposites, like trying to make a heavy locomotive move slowly down a steep hill. A pitcher has to go through all the motions of throwing a fastball, and then somehow make his change-up go slow. Here's how to do it.

The change-up is held and thrown exactly like a fastball until the ball passes in front of the pitcher's head. The moment his arm moves in front of his head, a number of things happen. Instead of the pitcher's wrist moving ahead of his elbow, as it does with a fastball, the reverse occurs. The pitcher's elbow shoots ahead of his wrist and is yanked almost straight down. This

This dissipates much of the body's built-up power; the ball is thrown with only the forearm and wrist (C), resulting in a soft, slow pitch (D).

C   D

motion forces the pitcher to merely flip the ball with his forearm and wrist without the additional strength of his shoulder and upper arm. Although he is throwing the ball as hard as he can, the ball goes much slower than normal. The batter sees the pitcher's arm moving as fast as it would with a fastball and will adjust his swing accordingly, only to be fooled by the pitch. Generally, a change-up should be thrown very low so that it passes across the plate as a ball or a very low strike. It should never be thrown higher than a batter's knees or on the inside of the plate.

A change-up is a pitch that should ideally be thrown when a batter is guessing fastball and is inclined to swing. Therefore, it is a perfect pitch to throw when the pitcher is behind the batter in count—say, two balls and no strikes—and the batter has the go-ahead sign from his coach. It is the kind of pitch that gets the pitcher out of ticklish situations with one throw, since it is usually weakly hit.

THE SCREWBALL

A screwball—the pitch—got its name because it must be thrown in a way that is the opposite of every other pitch; because the ball spins in a way that

The Screwball's Movement Relative to a Right-Handed Batter.
The screwball to a right-handed batter tails up and in, toward the fists, making it a difficult pitch to hit.

is the reverse of a curveball; and, finally, because only a demented person would specialize in such a perverse pitch that is so hard to master and so damaging to a pitcher's arm.

The first great screwball pitcher was Carl Hubbell, a lifetime 253-game winner with the New York Giants between 1928 and 1943. Hubbell, known as "King Carl" and "the Meal Ticket," fanned Babe Ruth, Lou Gehrig, and Jimmie Foxx in succession in the 1934 All-Star game, all with his baffling screwball. Hubbell threw as many as 100 screwballs per game, and by his late twenties his throwing arm was twisted permanently in such a way that when it hung limp alongside his body, the palm of his throwing hand would be facing away from his body.

Over the years few pitchers have tried to master the screwball, and even those who have, have used it as a third or fourth pitch to offset their fastball, curve, change-up, and slider rather than as their bread-and-butter pitch. Even Fernando Valenzuela, the Dodgers' fine pitcher who won the Cy Young Award in his rookie year (1981), seldom throws more than 50 or 60 screwballs a game. The pitch exerts a terrible pressure on the shoulder and elbow joints of the throwing arm. It is also the most difficult pitch to master

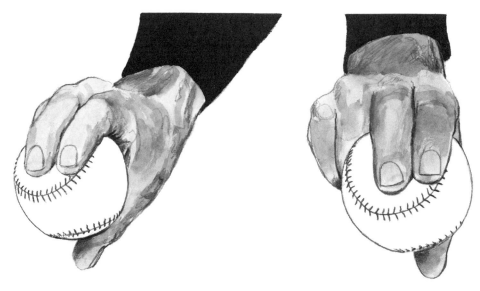

The Screwball Grip.
The ball is gripped along the inside of the long seams.

Throwing the Screwball

The motion begins the same as for a fastball (A), but as the arm passes in front of the ear, it turns in a counterclockwise direction (B), which gives the ball its spin. Instead of finishing across the body, as it normally would, the arm finishes to the body's extreme right (C).

A

because to throw it a pitcher must learn to reverse everything he has ever learned about throwing a curveball, which, in itself, is a tough pitch to master. Throwing a screwball is akin to making a clock tick backwards to tell time. Yet the pitch does not behave radically different from a curveball. In fact, it behaves exactly like a curveball except that it breaks in the opposite direction. The advantage to throwing it lies in the fact that a right-handed pitcher facing a left-handed batter (and vice versa) can now throw a breaking ball that moves away from the batter instead of in on him, which is what happens with the standard curveball. A pitcher like Valenzuela with a good curveball and a great screwball thus becomes devastating. He can keep any batter off stride with the knowledge that he can break a ball in on him or away from him at will.

B   C

A screwball is thrown just like a fastball until the point at which the pitcher's arm is passing alongside his head. However, a screwball is not held like a curveball. Instead of placing his two fingers side by side against the seam, as he does when throwing a curveball, the pitcher must place them side by side in the opposite direction, so that he will force the seams to spin in the opposite direction when he twists his wrist and arm. That is how the screwball gets its break. As the arm moves forward past the ear, the pitcher begins to turn his wrist and arm in a counterclockwise manner so that when his arm follows through, it moves away from his body from right to extreme right, instead of crossing his body right to left. The ball will approach the plate spinning in a manner opposite to that of a curveball, and its break, when thrown by a

The screwball, when thrown too often and too hard, can take its toll on a pitcher's arm. Fernando Valenzuela of the Dodgers rarely throws more than 60 screwballs a game. Note the twist of his arm as he releases the pitch.

right-handed pitcher, will be down and away to a left-handed batter. The screwball is difficult to hit, not because its movement is so unusual by itself but because its movement is so unusual in relation to the pitcher throwing it. For example, batters are used to right-handers throwing breaking balls that move right to left, and so a reverse breaking ball brings an element of surprise and oddity with it.

Why and when does a young pitcher begin to experiment with a screwball? The question can't be answered. Who can say why a pitcher like Valenzuela began to throw the pitch and, even more unexplainable, why he mastered it at such an early age. Most young pitchers spend years trying to master the basic pitches with little success, much less try to master such a difficult and confusing pitch as the screwball.

THE FORKBALL

The forkball gets its name from the way it is held in a pitcher's hand. The first two fingers are spread like the prongs of a fork, and the ball is jammed in between the fingers. Like the knuckleball, the forkball is a "trick" pitch, so named because the manner in which it moves to the plate is unpredictable, magical: a trick.

There is no explanation for the behavior of either a forkball or a knuckleball; they seldom follow the same pattern from pitch to pitch. Either pitch is capable of dipping, rising, sailing, breaking to the left or right, or maybe all of those things on its way toward the plate. The forkball, however, is a bit more consistent than a knuckleball. It generally breaks downward, though not always. Also, like the knuckleball, it does not spin much on its way to the plate. Indeed, it looks as if it is floating in a vacuum—a butterfly in the wind. It's unpredictable. One of the most famous forkball pitchers of all time was Elroy Face, a reliever with the Pittsburgh Pirates during the fifties and sixties. Elroy

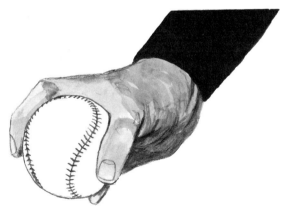

The Forkball Grip.
It is easier to control if you're long-fingered.

A

Throwing the Forkball

The motion is the same as for a fastball
(A), but the wrist is kept stiff, the elbow
shoots slightly forward (B), and the wrist
is then snapped down (C). This usually
causes the pitch to drop as it approaches
the plate.

was a little man, without much natural talent, and so he was forced to develop this trick pitch in order to survive. Survive he did, in the big leagues for 16 years; in fact, he still holds the record for best winning percentage in a season of any pitcher. In 1959, Face won eighteen straight games without a loss before finally losing his last decision of the year, finishing at 18–1. Not bad for a little guy who supposedly could not break a pane of glass with his fastball from a distance of three feet. In fact, that's why Face lasted so long as a reliever, a trade that usually takes such a toll on its practitioners that they seldom last more than five years in the majors. Face was able to last because his forkball, like a knuckleball, took very little toll on his arm.

The forkball is a pitch that should be thrown just like a fastball, only at less than full speed and with a stiff wrist until just before the moment of release. Then the wrist is snapped forward and down, propelling the ball toward the plate.

If the forkball is such an easy pitch to throw, why don't more pitchers throw it? The answer is twofold. First, a pitcher must have long fingers to be able to grasp the ball properly. Second, he must be willing to undergo years of torment, as Phil Niekro did with his knuckleball, before he can even hope to begin to master such a baffling pitch. The pitch goes where it wants to, and it takes some pitchers years to learn to surrender to its will.

B

C

THE KNUCKLEBALL

In 1959, when I was a hard-throwing rookie on the McCook Braves of the Class-D Nebraska State League, Phil Niekro was the tenth pitcher on our ten-man staff. Each day we all expected Phil to get his unconditional release. Not because he was untalented (because even then he possessed a baffling knuckleball) but because he was so unable to control the pitch's flight that he began to despair of it, and so resorted to throwing only fastballs and curves, which, in his case, weren't sufficient to get batters out. The pitch was so unpredictable that it was driving Phil mad. When he got it over the plate it was unhittable. (Years later, as a successful big-league pitcher with the Atlanta

Veteran pitcher Phil Niekro seemed to push his knuckleball off his fingers rather than throw it. The pitch's unpredictable movement makes it difficult to control.

Braves, Phil once struck out Richie Allen of the Phillies four times in a row. Allen just took his desultory three swings each time at the plate and walked back to the dugout smiling. When asked why he didn't try harder against Niekro's knuckleball, Allen responded, "I don't want to mess up my swing trying to hit that pitch.") However, more often than not, Phil's knuckleball would dart hither and yon, eluding not only the batter and the umpire but also the catcher. If trying to hit a knuckleball is akin to swatting a fly with a blade of grass, trying to catch it, or call it for a strike, is equally as difficult.

Phil Niekro spent almost seven years in the minor leagues trying to control his knuckleball, and only when he stopped trying to control it, surrendering to its will rather than trying to impose his will on it, did he reach the major leagues, where he won more than 300 games. Phil simply decided to let the pitch lead him where it might. One year it led him to 23 major-league victories. The next year Phil decided to throw his knuckleball with more speed, and the result was 18 major-league losses. He shrugged, and decided again never to try to impose his will on the pitch. It takes that kind of temperament to be a

The Knuckleball Grip

The ball is actually gripped along the seams with the fingernails rather than the knuckles. The first joint of the thumb grips the lower seam.

knuckleball pitcher. It is not a pitch for emotional types like Goose Gossage or ex Mets and Phillies great Tug McGraw, but rather for those patient, long-suffering guys like Niekro and Hoyt Wilhelm, guys who are willing to spend years learning a simple lesson: once a knuckleball leaves a pitcher's hand, it does what it wants.

The term "knuckleball" is a misnomer, since all great knuckleball pitchers, like Niekro, grip the ball with their fingernails, which dig into the ball's seams, not their knuckles. The ball is not so much thrown as pushed toward the batter, as if the pitcher were trying to push a sticky door closed. The result should be a pitch that barely spins at all, that is caught in invisible wind currents that make it perform a host of tricks on its way to the plate. The pitch must be thrown at a nice, easy speed, not too hard or too easy or it will not perform —which is why most pitchers spend so many years trying to master it. What they are trying to find is that ideal speed at which their pitch will perform. One of the advantages of the knuckleball is that it takes very little out of a pitcher's arm. Wilhelm pitched in the majors almost to the age of 50, as did Niekro who retired at age 48.

Throwing the Knuckleball

The ball is pushed with minimal wrist snap, causing it to float, rather than spin, toward the plate.

THE CATCHER'S SIGNS

The relationship between a pitcher and his catcher is an unusual one. On the one hand, the pitcher has the final responsibility for the pitches he throws; yet, on the other hand, the catcher's choice of pitches plays an important part in that decision. I remember once, in the minor leagues, I shook off my catcher's signs three times before he finally called for the pitch I wanted to throw. No matter how strongly he felt I should throw *his* pitch, the final responsibility lay with me. I had to throw the pitch I was comfortable with. Of course, it didn't help matters that my catcher was also my manager, Jim Fanning, who later

became general manager of the Montreal Expos. My shaking off his signs did not help my career over the long run, even though I did strike out the batter with the pitch I had wanted to throw all along. Other pitchers, more successful than I, have shown greater confidence in their catchers, and it has helped their careers immeasurably. Here is Tom Seaver talking about his relationship with Jerry Grote, his catcher with the Mets during the seventies:

"I couldn't do more than I was physically or mentally capable of on the mound. If I tried to throw harder than I could, the ball went slower than it normally would. I couldn't fabricate conclusions in my mind about how to pitch to a batter if my mind wasn't ready for them. I couldn't force things.

104

Sometimes in a game I'd concentrate so hard on my motion, trying to get it right, that I had nothing left for the batter. Then I let Grote call my pitches. I just responded physically. I surrendered that mental load to Grote, and it was one less load I had to worry about. When I got my motion organized, I'd take that load back."

Just what are those signs a Grote flashes to a Seaver, and what do they mean? From a crouch, a catcher usually uses hand signals to indicate to the pitcher what he wants him to throw. A pitcher responds to those signs either with a nod of his head (yes) or a shake (no), or with a slight flick of his glove, which also indicates no. The catcher's signs in their simplest form can be just numbers. The catcher flattens his ungloved hand along the inside of his thigh and then raises one, two, or three of his fingers to indicate a pitch, the number indicating the pitch having been agreed upon before the game—for example

Sign-Giving: The Catcher

The catcher conceals his finger signals with his thigh and glove. A touch to either thigh can indicate the desired location of a pitch.

one finger equals fastball, two fingers equal curveball. Often a change-up is indicated by the catcher wiggling his fingers.

With a runner on second base, a catcher often changes his signs, making them more complicated so that the runner looking in on him cannot steal the sign and flash it in some way to the batter. In this instance, a catcher might flash three signs in quick succession with the knowledge that he and the pitcher have agreed that only the second sign, say, is the one to be decided upon. Whatever sign is agreed upon, however, the pitcher must always bear in mind that the final responsibility for the pitch is his. He, not the catcher, gets the win or loss alongside his name at the end of the game, and so he must throw the pitch he feels most comfortable with. Trusting his catcher's judgment is one thing, but throwing a pitch he has no confidence in at the catcher's request is another. No self-respecting pitcher should ever do that.

3

The Pitchers

Pitchers are unique among baseball players. Only they are credited with a win or loss at the end of a game. To withstand that pressure, they must have monumental egos. They must want to control the action, not flee from the responsibility. Although big egos are not rare in sports, the kind of massive ego a pitcher must have in order to step onto a mound before thousands of fans, all waiting for him to deliver the ball, is unlike that in any other sport. Here, during his prime, is Tom Seaver, a perfect example of the breed, talking about his craft:

"If I couldn't pitch, I'd do something else. It wouldn't bother me much. But if I *could* pitch and I wasn't, that would bother me. That would bother me a lot. Pitching is what makes me happy. I've devoted my life to it. I live my life around the five days between starts. It determines what I eat, when I go to bed, what I do when I'm awake. It determines how I spend my life when not pitching. If it means in the winter I eat cottage cheese instead of chocolate chip cookies to keep my weight down, then I eat cottage cheese. I might want those cookies, but I won't ever eat them. That might bother some people, but it doesn't bother me. I enjoy that cottage cheese more than I would

107

Talent, poise, discipline, and desire have combined to make Jack Morris a brilliant, successful pitcher.

A blazing fastball and a solid, beautifully-controlled curve, have made Dwight Gooden one of the best pitchers in the major league today.

those cookies because I know it'll help me do what makes me happy. Life isn't very heavy for me. I'm happy when I pitch well, so I only do those things that make me happy. Pitching is the whole thing for me. I want to prove I'm the best ever."

If Seaver was an exception as a pitcher, it was partly in his extreme dedication to his craft along with his physical talent. It was this dedication, as well as his intelligence, that made him one of the greatest pitchers who ever lived. To a greater or lesser degree, every pitcher must have this kind of dedication.

There are three types of pitchers in the major leagues today: starting pitchers, long relievers, and short relievers, or "stoppers," as they are called. The stopper's job is to stop cold an opposing team's late-inning rally. A long reliever usually appears early on in a game, when the starting pitcher has faltered, and it is his job to hold the opposition scoreless through the middle innings so that his team can get back in the game. The starter's job, naturally, is to begin the game and, if possible, pitch at least six or seven good innings before turning over the game to the stopper.

Each of these pitchers needs a specific kind of talent, both mental and physical. A starter, for example, needs at least three good pitches to carry him through the long haul of seven innings, during which he must face each opposing batter at least three times. He is like a patient novelist, churning out his pages, his scoreless innings, time after time, with the vision to sustain himself to the end. Starters tend to be disciplined, rational, plodding fellows who can pace themselves over the long haul. They can give up a run or two in the early innings without panicking, without abandoning their game plan.

Long relievers are generally second-line starting pitchers who for one reason or another are not able to crack the starting rotation. They generally have only two good pitches in their arsenal, which is enough to make them successful during the middle innings, when they might have to face each opposing batter twice.

Short relievers, like Goose Gossage, Jeff Reardon, and Dan Quisenberry, are the glamor boys of pitching. Short relievers are to starting pitchers what mad poets are to plodding novelists. They are not dull, disciplined fellows who see their profession in terms of games, victories, and seasons. They are ephemeral creatures, noted for brief, blinding flashes of brilliance that have more to do with their emotions than their intellects. They see their jobs in terms of a single pitch, a single batter, an out, rarely more than an inning or two. This ability to compress all of their emotional and physical energies into such a short time span (a starter, on the other hand, can coast through lazy early innings while the fans warm to their beer and the batters try to unlimber their muscles) often leaves short relievers emotionally drained after their job is done. To store up their energies for their late-inning appearances, they often sleep in the bullpen during the game, play cards, tell tales—do anything but concentrate on the action until just before they are called on to enter it. A starting pitcher has only to worry about one game every five days. A short reliever, however, is like a doctor on constant call. He may pitch two, three, four days in a row, as many as 90 games in a year. He must have a resilient arm capable of springing back quickly after work, and he must be able to warm up in minutes, sometimes after only a dozen pitches or so. Often, this is why their job is so ephemeral. Short relief puts a terrible strain on their pitching arms.

Short relievers need just one excellent pitch rather than three or four adequate pitches, and often it is a trick pitch. Sutter's split-fingered fastball, Quisenberry's submarine pitch, Hoyt Wilhelm's knuckleball, Elroy Face's forkball—these are characteristic pitches for the short reliever. Still, there are short relievers with conventional pitches, like Jeff Reardon with his high-90s fastball.

Short relievers are emotional types, a little "flaky," in baseball parlance, the kind of guys who constantly have to boost their own egos because they never had the kind of overwhelming, broad-ranged talent that starters like Jack Morris have. To prove to themselves and to others that they have confidence

Mike Scott's success as a starter owes largely to his mastery of a sinking pitch, the split-fingered fastball.

in themselves, short relievers often go through a great show of emotion on the mound. Tug McGraw jumped up and down like a child after a good pitch. He pounded his glove, talked out loud. Al Hrabosky, the "Mad Hungarian" of St. Louis Cardinal fame, used to walk around, exorting himself out loud before each pitch, and then spring back to the mound, all psyched up. Gossage grumbles and curses, and kicks the dirt, and looks constantly angered at some imagined slight he is suffering.

And yet . . . for all their emotion, short relievers are a fatalistic lot. As McGraw used to say, "Sometimes you're gonna get lit up. That's it. You just gotta admit the batter did his job and forget it."

How does a pitcher decide which career he is going to follow? He doesn't. Often it is dictated to him by his talent, or lack of it, and by the opinions of the baseball people around him. Gossage began his career with the White Sox as a starting pitcher, but he had only one great pitch, his fastball, and so, before long, he was relegated to the bullpen. Some young pitchers can never adjust to either a starting job or a short-relief job. Emotional types with a host of pitches still make poor starters, while plodding, rational types with one great pitch still make poor short relievers, because they can't psych themselves up quickly enough to do their job. It takes them too long to warm to the action, and by then the game is lost. It is rare when a young pitcher can change his emotional nature to fit the job he has been assigned—but it can happen.

4

Setting Up the Batter

The contest between the batter and the pitcher hinges upon the pitcher's ability to keep the batter mentally off stride. A pitcher does this by varying the speed and position of his pitches. Some power pitchers can be successful merely by overpowering batters with blazing fastballs and curveballs that fall off the table. But those pitchers are the exception. The pitcher with more modest stuff must rely on cunning and control to outduel the batter.

In general, a pitcher will try to keep the ball low and away from the batter, with an occasional high-and-inside pitch thrown for effect. Unless a pitcher has exceptional speed, a high-and-inside fastball should be thrown to force the hitter back from the plate, not necessarily to make him swing at the pitch. No matter how weak a batter is, if he is thrown nothing but a steady diet of low-and-away pitches, sooner or later he'll adjust his swing and hit one of them.

The ratio of fastballs to curveballs to sliders to change-ups a pitcher throws each game should be determined not only by which pitches are generally his best but also by which pitches are working best for him that day. If a pitcher has an excellent curveball on a certain day, he should not work it to death, but save it for his toughest situa-

113

By mixing both the speed and the location of his pitches, Dave Righetti of the Yankees keeps batters guessing.

tions. Neither should a pitcher ever abandon his weakest pitch on a given day; he should try to use it in certain spots to keep a batter off balance—not necessarily to get him to swing at it. Thus, a pitcher should "show" a batter his weakest stuff but throw it to a spot, say, off the plate, where he can't hit it. A curveball in the dirt reminds the batter that the pitcher possesses such a pitch while still not giving him a chance to hit it. It is one more pitch the batter must think about.

No matter whether the batter is a fastball hitter or a curveball hitter, in a crisis the pitcher must go with his strength, even if that strength is also the batter's strength. Thus, even against Don Mattingly, a fastball hitter, Roger Clemens will go mainly with his fastball. He will have a better chance of retiring Mattingly with his fastball than Mattingly will have of hitting it. At best, major-league hitters hit in only three out of ten chances at bat. The percentages are in the pitcher's favor.

If a pitcher discovers a batter's blind spot—a spot where the batter seems incapable of hitting the ball—he should not work that spot to death. He should save it for ideal situations. Any batter, no matter how weak, who is thrown every pitch to his blind spot will soon learn to hit those pitches. Also, if a batter has a strong spot, a pitcher should not abandon that spot forever. He should wait for an ideal situation and then try to get the batter out with a pitch to his strong spot.

If a batter swings and misses a bad pitch, the pitcher should throw the next pitch in the same spot—only more so. In other words, if a batter swings at a shoulder-level fastball and misses it, the pitcher should throw the next pitch at the batter's eye level. If again the batter swings and misses, the pitcher should throw the next one even higher and see what happens. He may have discovered the batter's blind spot.

When a pitcher is ahead of a batter in the count—say, two strikes and one ball—he should try to get the batter to swing at a bad pitch off the plate. When, on the other hand, the pitcher is behind the batter—say, two balls and no strikes— he will have to throw a strike, and it should be the type of pitch the batter is least expecting. An off-speed pitch—slider, curveball, or change-up—is most effective, since batters generally look for fastballs when they are ahead of the pitchers in the count.

The farther ahead of a batter a pitcher is, the more pitches he can waste in setting up his opponent for his "out" pitch. For instance, with two strikes and no balls on a batter, a pitcher may waste two successive high-and-inside fastballs to set up a low-and-outside curveball, or he may throw two low-and-outside curveballs to set up a high-and-inside fastball.

Generally, a free-swinging power hitter like Mark McGwire can be fooled if the pitcher varies the speed of his pitches. A base hitter like Wade Boggs can be gotten out by the pitcher's changing the type and location of pitches—fastball to slider to curveball over different corners of the plate. A weak hitter can be gotten out mostly with fastballs and sliders, and should rarely be thrown an off-speed pitch. Usually he's weak because his swing is too slow—he can't get his bat around quickly enough on fastballs—but an off-speed pitch is just the kind of slow pitch he can adjust to.

I remember the first time I went to spring training with the then Milwaukee Braves, in 1960. I was a wild, hard-throwing rookie pitcher who had been told, repeatedly, by the Braves' front office that I had to become "a pitcher, not a thrower" before I could make the big leagues. I took those words to heart the first time I appeared on the mound in an intersquad game that spring. Most of the batters had just arrived in camp, while we pitchers had already been there throwing for two weeks. We were far ahead of the batters, whose rusty swings had yet to be unlimbered by more than a few moments of batting practice. I was wild that day, as usual, and in the first inning I found myself with the bases loaded and a left-handed batter coming up. To this day, I don't remember his name. He was just a journeyman Triple-A player trying to catch on with the Braves. He was already into his thirties, while I was not yet twenty years old. Facing him, I thought of all those comments from the Braves' front office, so the very first pitch I threw him was a change-up. His swing was so late that he timed the pitch perfectly and knocked it over the right-field fence. He was laughing all the way around the bases, as were most of the Braves in the dugout, at the idiocy of such a hard-throwing pitcher doing the batter a favor by tossing him a spring training change-up. The next day I was on a bus to the Braves' minor-league camp in Waycross, Georgia. But I had learned my lesson. Never give a weak hitter or a rusty one a straight change-up when you have a good fastball. Save the change-up for the strong hitters.

TWO HYPOTHETICAL SITUATIONS

Now let's see how a hypothetical pitcher (right-handed, good fastball, curve, change-up, and slider) would pitch to two modern classics of big-league hitting, Reggie Jackson and Pete Rose. Let's assume the pitcher's best pitch is his fastball, while his curveball is good, as are his slider and change-up.

Reggie Jackson

A muscular free-swinger who liked the ball out over the plate so he could extend his arms and use their power, Reggie Jackson was tightly muscled through the shoulders and chest, so his mobility on a hard inside pitch was always suspect, even in his prime. Let's bring Reg up to the plate and see how our hypothetical pitcher would have worked him.

1st pitch: Slow curveball on the outside corner of the plate for a strike. Reggie liked to hit the fastball and could hit the curveball only after he had seen it a few times and adjusted his swing. So give him a curveball first pitch, get him thinking about it, and don't throw another one for a strike again.

2nd pitch: Another curveball, this time low and inside, in the dirt, if necessary, to Reggie, a left-handed hitter. Now, he's thinking, with the count 1 and 1, that he's going to see nothing but breaking balls. He adjusts his thinking to breaking balls.

3rd pitch: Fastball low and on the outside corner for a strike. This should catch Reggie flat-footed, unable to pull the trigger on a pitch he likes to hit. Now he's talking to himself: Wait until the pitcher tries to get that fastball by me again!

4th pitch: Another fastball, low and far outside. Reggie strides toward it, but it is too far off the plate for him to swing. He's literally grinding his bat in his hands now, hoping the pitcher will throw that pitch over the plate next time.

5th pitch: With the count at 2 and 2, the pitcher fires what looks like a fastball right down the heart of the plate, waist-high. Reggie strides toward it with his big, muscular, sweeping swing. But halfway into the pitch, the ball, a slider, darts in toward his belt buckle. It is too late for him to adjust. He hits the ball off the handle of the bat, a weak fly ball to the first baseman.

Pete Rose

A slap hitter, Peter Rose used to hit the ball wherever it was pitched. He tried to keep it on the ground, get it through the infield, because he did not have the power to hit the ball far in the air. A pesky hitter who hunched low over the plate, thereby diminishing the pitcher's strike zone, Pete was an excellent fastball hitter in his day and only a fair breaking-ball hitter. He was a tough man to fool at the plate. Let's bring him up and have him bat left-handed here.

1st pitch: Fastball in on the fists for a strike. Pete didn't expect that (in his prime he was a great fastball hitter). He's determined not to be fooled again. But that's the last fastball for a strike he's going to see from this pitcher.

2nd pitch: Another fastball, in low, almost hitting Pete's feet. He has to skip away from the pitch. The count is 1 and 1.

3rd pitch: Sharp curveball aimed for the middle of the plate and breaking down and in on Pete. He swings, gets a good piece of it but fouls it off on the ground behind first base. Count: 1 ball and 2 strikes.

4th pitch: Fastball up and in on Pete. It's so close it forces him back off the plate. He's thinking to himself: Now just throw that SOB over the plate! Count: 2 and 2.

5th pitch: Straight change-up low and on the outside corner of the plate. Pete commits himself too soon, makes contact, but just lofts a lazy fly ball to left-center field. He flings his bat down in disgust and races, à la Charlie Hustle of his playing days, toward first base before the ball is caught. He swings toward his dugout cursing himself.

Again, remember: Keep the batter guessing. Change speeds and spots continually. Don't ever let the batter set himself in the batter's box with the knowledge of what pitch is coming to what spot. A pitcher with only modest ability who keeps the batter guessing can succeed, while a pitcher who has superior ability but is obvious and predictable will be less successful.

The distinctive batting styles of a Reggie Jackson and a Pete Rose are two of many styles that a pitcher must face—and seek to overcome.

5

Pitching to Situations

With no one on base, the pitcher's first concern is to throw strikes. He will be less accurate in regard to the corners of the plate than he would be with a runner on third base. His objective is to throw the ball over the plate until the batters prove to him that this is not enough, that he must be closer with his control. No matter how feeble a pitcher feels his fastball may be, he should throw it until batters prove they can hit it. In the twilight of his career, Robin Roberts, the great Phillies pitcher, once pitched a shutout with a fastball that seemed to creep up to the plate. Yet Roberts believed he could get batters out with that fastball, and he did.

With a runner on first base and one or none out, a pitcher should try to keep his pitches low in the hope that the batter will hit a ground ball into a double play. The pitcher should lead this batter off with a straight overhand curve in the hope that he will be swinging on the first pitch. All down-breaking pitches are harder for a batter to hit into the air.

With a runner on second base only, a pitcher can be extra fine with the batter. If he walks him, he will set up the possibility of either a force play at any base or a double play. This is the one circumstance when to walk a batter is almost prefera-

119

With men on base, a pitcher's responsibilities double. Now he throws from the stretch position to keep the runners from advancing while he tries to retire the batter.

ble to giving him anything good to hit. This is the ideal situation in that the pitcher can now throw his best stuff in the finest spots without worrying about walking the batter.

With a runner on third base and none or one out, the pitcher must try to get the batter out, either on a strikeout or a ground ball. A fly ball to the outfield will score the run as easily as a base hit will. (It is a good idea with runners on base for the pitcher to let the infielders know what pitches he is throwing —a curveball, a fastball, or whatever. There should be some signal to them from either the catcher or the pitcher. This will help them play the hitters.)

With a runner on first, and the batter obviously planning to bunt him over to second, a pitcher should try to keep his pitches, mainly fastballs, up and in on the batter in the hope that the batter will pop the ball up to the catcher. If the pitcher is not sure whether the batter is going to bunt, he can try to find out by throwing a pitchout, and hope the batter tips his hand. Or he can simply step off the rubber at the last possible second before delivering a pitch. Often, a batter will indicate what he is planning on doing with a slight movement of the bat even before the pitcher delivers.

With a runner on second base and the batter trying to move him to third by hitting the ball to the right side of the infield, the pitcher should try to keep the ball up and in on a right-handed batter and low and away to a lefty. This should force the batter to hit the ball to the left side of the infield, allowing the fielders to make a play at third base and get the lead runner.

When a starting pitcher finds himself with a lead of four runs or better, he should make a point of throwing strikes at all costs in the later innings. He doesn't have to be too fine now, since it will take a big inning to defeat him, and big innings rarely come with five consecutive hits. Usually, they are sandwiched around a few walks. A pitcher should always remember this cardinal rule: The closer the score, the finer a pitcher has to be; the greater the score in his favor, the less fine he has to be. Again, big innings usually come not from five or six consecutive hits but from a few walks sandwiched around a big hit or two. Make the batters hit their way on base—don't give them a free pass.

During the course of a game you may find that your pitches fluctuate from inning to inning. In the early innings you might have an excellent fastball and only a mediocre curveball. Then try to get most of your outs with the fastball, but don't just abandon the curve. Pick your spots, show the batter the pitch to keep him guessing. Then, in the later innings, if your curveball comes around and you lose a bit off your fastball, reverse your pitching strategy. In this way, over a nine-inning game, you become, really, two pitchers. Don't be afraid to adjust your style according to what is working for you at the moment. Let your talent dictate how you pitch. Don't try to impose your will on your talent. If your fastball isn't much during the early innings, use it as a waste pitch, and get your outs with your breaking ball, or vice versa.

In the late innings of a one-run game you are leading, remember, at all costs: Keep that first batter of the inning off base. Still, make him hit good hard stuff. Try not to make a mistake with an off-speed pitch in the later innings of a close game. I remember a game I pitched in the minor leagues. I was leading 3–2 in the ninth inning, with two outs and a runner on first base. I had a 3 and 2 count on the batter and hung a curveball to him. He belted a game-winning home run he never would have hit if I had gone with my fastball. If a batter is going to beat you in the late innings, make him beat you with your best pitch, whatever it is. Don't be too cute!

With runners on base, a pitcher must repeatedly decide what he will do with the ball when and if it is hit back to him—and he must decide this before the pitch, not after it, when it is too late. He should make an automatic habit of this because once he focuses his attention on his pitching, nothing should interfere with his concentration on setting up and dispatching the batter. A pitcher is first of all a pitcher and must devote most of his energies and concentration to each pitch. Everything else is secondary—fielding bunts, throwing to the right base, and so forth.

Also, a pitcher should never alter the pattern of his pitching to satisfy a catcher or infielder. For instance, with a runner on first base who has a good chance of stealing second on the next pitch, a catcher likes to call for fastballs, which get to him more quickly and are easier to handle, giving him a better chance to throw out the runner stealing. However, a pitcher's first duty is to retire the batter, and often it will do him no good whatsoever to try to help his catcher. If he accommodates him, the result is often a hit to the outfield on a fastball the pitcher knew he shouldn't have thrown.

No matter what the situation, a pitcher should never let up physically or mentally, but should always throw his best stuff. If you always throw with your best, most natural motion, control should come naturally. But don't sacrifice your best pitches for control. For instance, with the bases loaded and a 3-and-2 count on the batter, throw your best pitch now, not just a pitch you hope will be a strike. It is better to walk the batter than to throw a mediocre pitch that might be solidly hit. If there is one cardinal rule for a pitcher, it is: Win or lose, make sure you give them your best.

Still, you can't forget Tug McGraw's old saying: Sooner or later every one gets lit up. Hits are going to fall, and when they do, you'd better know where to be on the field to back up a play. Here are some cardinal rules a pitcher should follow during action swirling around him.

1. On all weakly hit balls to the right side of the infield, the pitcher should move toward first base. If the ball is caught by the first baseman too far from the bag, the pitcher will have to take the throw. Even if the first baseman doesn't

On a ball hit weakly to the right side of the infield, the pitcher should run on an angled route to first base for the possible throw.

catch the ball, and it is caught by the second baseman, often the first baseman finds himself too far from the bag to take the throw, and again the pitcher has to cover. The best way for a pitcher to cover first base is to run on a straight line toward a point on the foul line about fifteen feet from the bag, and then, just as he reaches the line, turn sharply left, running up to the bag, where he can take the throw.

2. On all plays at second base or third base, the pitcher should back up third base. He should position himself about twenty feet behind the bag in direct

On plays at second or third, the pitcher should back up third base, positioning himself twenty feet behind the bag and in line with the incoming throw.

On plays at the plate, the pitcher should back up the catcher, twenty feet behind the plate and in direct line with the throw.

line with the incoming throw, in case it is wild.

   3. On all plays at the plate, the pitcher should back up the catcher, again about twenty feet behind him in direct line with the incoming throw.

Conditioning and Injuries

A pitcher's career is more fragile than the career of any other baseball player because he is more susceptible to physical injuries, and those injuries are more damaging to his talent than they would be to any other player's. A pitcher has to operate as close as possible to 100 percent, physically, or his talent will suffer. An outfielder, for example, can play with a pulled hamstring muscle. True, it will limit his range in the field, and his speed on the bases, but still he will be able to hit well enough, and so play the game. A pitcher with a pulled hamstring will never take the mound. Depending on which leg the pull is in, he will either not be able to push off the rubber or will be unable to land in his follow-through with his full momentum.

Furthermore, a pitcher is more active than any other player. He is performing at peak intensity on every pitch, and his talent rests primarily with his arm, which is the most fragile of all ballplayers' physical parts. The human arm was not designed to throw 130 pitches a game. Pitching is a terrible wrenching motion, and it is a miracle that pitchers have been able to accomplish so much over so many years. In fact, most pitchers pitch with a bit of soreness every game of their

125

To help avoid pulled muscles and other injuries, the smart pitcher includes stretching in his conditioning and warmup program.

careers. For them, pain is a fact of life. All pitchers must learn quickly to distinguish a natural soreness from a potential injury. Often, young pitchers tend to quit throwing whenever they feel any soreness in their arms. The standard rule for pitchers and any athletes should be: If the pain gets worse, stop working immediately; but if it stays the same or begins to diminish as you work, then it should not be regarded as serious.

Now, let's discuss three things: The muscles a pitcher is most likely to injure; the nature of those injuries; and how the injuries can be avoided, or diminished.

MUSCLES

The most obvious part of his body that a pitcher uses, and the most important, is his arm. Wonder! What else is new? Well, a pitcher's arm is really not just a single piece. It is made up of a number of different muscles, each of which can be strengthened or injured. Let's take a look at what those muscles are.

The biceps are the muscles on top of the arm, and the triceps are the muscles underneath. Although they are the muscles most needed to pull things toward you (biceps) or push things away from

**Anatomical View of
the Arm Muscles**

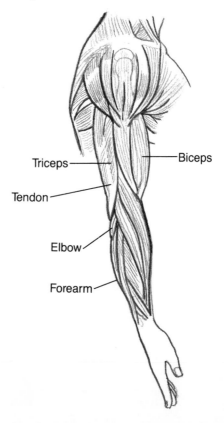

Triceps

Biceps

Tendon

Elbow

Forearm

muscles least likely to be injured when pitching. The forearm, from the elbow to the wrist, takes more of a beating than the biceps or triceps, and the elbow joint takes the most beating. The elbow is particularly susceptible to injury when throwing breaking balls (curveball, slider, screwball). The biceps and triceps are most susceptible to strains during spring training—often when a pitcher has a case of tendinitis, all he really has is a slight strain of the biceps or triceps, which reacts best to rest. The forearm is susceptible to injury when throwing both fastballs and breaking balls.

One of the most common injuries to a pitcher's elbow occurs when, over the years, bones chip away from the elbow and begin floating in the socket, causing the pitcher pain when he throws. These bone chips can sometimes be dissolved with injections, but most often they have to be removed by surgical means. Years ago this was a frightening experience, but not today. Pitchers come back almost to full capacity after elbow surgery a lot more frequently than they do after a shoulder operation.

The shoulder is probably where the pitcher most fears injury. A pitcher can still pitch, at diminished capacity, with any kind of arm injury except a shoulder injury. Pitchers with bad shoulders have been known to be unable to comb their hair or brush their teeth, much less throw a baseball. Hard-throwing overhand pitchers are particularly susceptible to shoulder injuries.

Muscles of the Shoulder

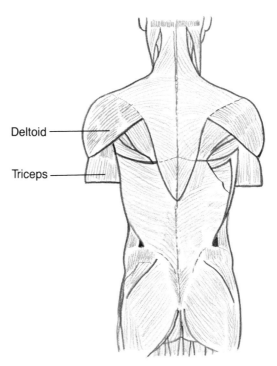

Deltoid

Triceps

The shoulder is really made up of three muscles: the front, side, and rear deltoid. These muscles overlap via a set of smaller shoulder muscles forming what is known as the rotator cuff. The dreaded rotator-cuff injury one hears so much about these days is either a tearing of one or more of these muscles or of one of the deltoid muscles from the bone. The best way to prevent this injury is to strengthen both sets of muscles so that they neither tear nor pull.

A pitcher's back muscles, from just under the rear of his shoulders all the way down to his buttocks, are also very important to his delivery. In this category I would include the upper back (latissimus dorsi) and the lower back, including the hips and the buttocks. A pitcher is more likely to injure his lower back, hips, or buttocks than he is his upper back, which is generally a big, strong muscle not that susceptible to injury. Tom Seaver was famous for coming up every spring with buttocks injuries and hip injuries which seriously hindered

Back and Buttock Muscles

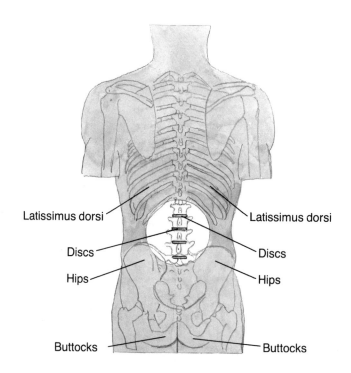

Muscles the Leg

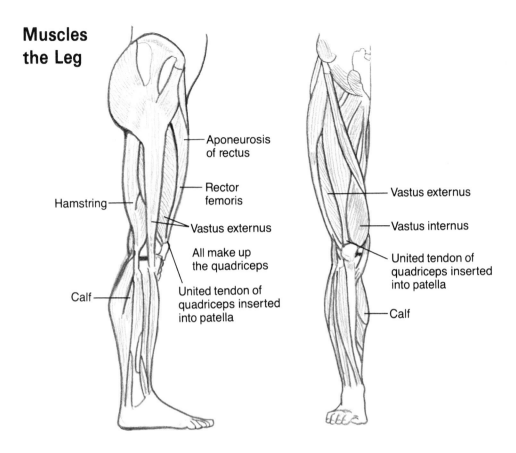

Aponeurosis of rectus

Rector femoris

Hamstring

Vastus externus

All make up the quadriceps

Calf

United tendon of quadriceps inserted into patella

Vastus externus

Vastus internus

United tendon of quadriceps inserted into patella

Calf

his push off the rubber and his follow-through. All of these muscles can be strengthened through proper exercise; injuries to the discs in the spinal column, however, can be repaired only through an operation.

Almost as important to his pitching as his arm are a pitcher's legs. If you don't think so, just try to throw the ball hard while standing flat-footed on the rubber without pushing forward. You'll lose at least 50 percent of your speed. It is that first push off the rubber that gives the pitcher his whole body momentum lunging toward the batter. For that, and the attendant follow-through, he needs strong, well-muscled legs. Again, Tom Seaver is an example of a pitcher whose legs seem noticeably more developed than any other part of his body.

The three most important parts of a pitcher's legs are the front, or quadriceps; the rear, or hamstrings; and the calf. Each of these sets of muscles can easily be strengthened to prevent injury and even to add to the force with which a pitcher drives off the rubber.

Now, let's talk about the exercises a pitcher can do that will help him prevent injuries.

EXERCISES

There are really only two kinds of exercises: strengthening exercises and flexibility exercises. The first makes muscles stronger and tighter, the second makes them longer and more flexible. Since every pitcher needs both strength and flexibility, he should perform those exercises that will do both things. Weight training is the perfect method for strengthening muscles, and calisthenics are perfect for flexibility. Ideally, a pitcher should perform weight training for a particular muscle and then offset that by following up immediately with some calisthenics. He should work out no more than twice a week, and never on successive days. The best place to work out is always in a gym, with the proper equipment.

A pitcher can never be too flexible. But he can become too muscular, so he must keep in mind that his weight training should be modest. His goal is not to become an Arnold Schwarzenegger, but simply to strengthen his muscles. A pitcher can become too tightly muscled, and this is why, before the sixties, weight training was frowned upon by most baseball people. Today, we are more enlightened, and we realize that a modest routine of lifting will not turn anyone into a musclebound hulk. Again, remember not to work your muscles more than twice a week, and never on successive days. When you lift

The Bicep Curl.

weights, what you are really doing is putting your muscles under stress. Your muscles then need at least 48 hours to restore themselves before the next bout of lifting.

Here are some basic terms and rules for weight lifting:

- A "repetition" is one complete movement of an exercise.
- A "set" is a series of repetitions done in succession before resting (e.g., ten reps and rest equal one set).
- The amount of weight to use for each exercise varies with each person. The best rule of thumb to follow is this: The weight should be light enough for you to perform at least six successive repetitions without cheating, and it should be heavy enough so that you can't perform more than fifteen repetitions too easily.
- Begin your weight training with light weights and then, after a month or so, increase the weights while maintaining the same number of repetitions.
- Expect a slight soreness the day after each workout. It is normal. Without it you aren't working hard enough.

The Bicep Curl

This exercise will strengthen your biceps. Stand with your legs slightly apart, holding either a barbell in both hands in front of you at your hips or a dumbbell in either hand at your sides. Now, keeping your elbows close to your sides, curl the bar, or the dumbbells, up to your neck, then lower them again

to their starting position. That's one repetition. Try to do at least three to five sets of bicep curls a workout, and try to do at least ten repetitions per set, but no more than fifteen.

The Tricep Press

Either seated or standing, grip a barbell in the center, hands about six to eight inches apart, or a dumbbell, as illustrated. Raise your hands directly over

The Tricep Press.

your head, then lower the weight behind your head, making sure to keep your elbows pointed up. Keeping your elbows rigid, press the weight upwards again using only your forearm from your elbow to your wrist. Again, perform the same sets and reps as for the bicep curl.

The Wrist Curl

This exercise should be performed seated. Grip a barbell as if you were going to perform a barbell curl, only position your hands much closer together,

The Wrist Curl.

about four inches apart. Now place your forearms on your thighs so that your wrists are off your knees. Now, using only your wrists, curl the barbell toward you as far as it can go. Do three sets of twelve reps, and then turn your arms around so that your hands are now on top of the bar, and perform the same exercise in reverse. Again, do three sets of twelve reps.

After performing each set of these exercises, you should shake your arms

Hanging from a Chinning Bar

Hanging helps stretch lifting-constricted muscles and keeps them loose.

to loosen them, and then hang perfectly still from a chinning bar for a count of ten to twenty seconds. This should loosen up the muscles you have just contracted.

The Deltoid Standing Lateral Raise

This is an excellent all-around shoulder exercise that will not tighten the shoulders too much so as to impair flexibility. For this you need two dumbbells. Stand with legs spread apart, leaning slightly forward from the waist up. Hold the dumbbells in front of you at arms' length, with palms facing each other, as illustrated. Now, swing the dumbbells up on each side of your body, with your arms bent in an L shape, until the dumbbells are at shoulder height. Hold them for a split second parallel to the floor before returning them slowly to the

The Deltoid Standing Lateral Raise.

starting position. Again, do three to five sets of twelve reps each.

To loosen up the deltoids after each set, again, hang freely from a chinning bar for a few seconds.

Hips, Buttocks, and Lower Back

The best exercise for all three of these body parts is called a hyperextension, and it requires no weights. It does require a hyperextension chair, however, which is usually found in a gym but seldom anywhere else. Position yourself so that you are facing the floor with your heels hooked under one leg of the hyperextension chair and your stomach on top of the other leg. Place your hands behind your head, and lean down as far as your upper body will go. Then, bring your upper body upward until it is parallel to the floor. Never go higher than this, since going higher risks injury to your lower back. Perform the entire motion slowly, and do at least ten to twenty reps for three sets.

To loosen up your muscles after this, perform a few toe-touching exercises,

Hyperextensions

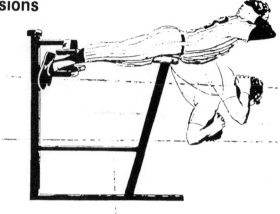

The Back and Leg Stretch

as follows. Stand with your feet together, and then, without bending your legs, reach down with both hands and grip your ankles. Hold that position for a count of ten, and then return upright. Do at least three sets of five reps of this.

Legs, Quadriceps, and Hamstrings

One of the best exercises for strengthening the front muscles of the upper leg (quadriceps), the rear muscles (hamstrings), and the buttocks and hips is,

simply, a squat. It is merely a deep knee bend performed with a weight on one's shoulders. It is the most basic of all weight-lifting exercises. Stand with your feet about shoulder-width apart, balance a barbell with a modest weight on your shoulders, and then squat down until your upper leg is parallel to the floor. It's important to keep your back straight and your head up on this exercise—if you lean either forward or backwards, you will lose your balance. Now, push upward until you are standing erect again. Try to do about ten reps for three to five sets for this exercise. Afterwards, stretch out your leg muscles by performing the same stretching exercises you did for your lower back.

The Calves

To strengthen your calves, simply stand with your toes on the edge of a stair and the rest of your foot off the stair. You'll need to hold on to something for balance. Now, let your body dip as far as it can without your toes slipping off the stair, then, using only your calf muscles, propel your body upright as far as it can go so that you are literally standing on your tiptoes. Do three sets of fifteen to twenty reps here since you are not using any weight other than your body weight.

Strengthening the Calves

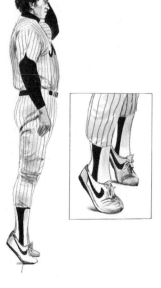

Again, the best way to loosen your calf muscles after this routine is to perform the same stretching exercises you did after your hyperextensions.

One final note about conditioning. Most pitching coaches believe a pitcher should do a lot of running to strengthen his legs. But the kind of light jogging they ask of a pitcher does very little to strengthen legs. The best kind of running is short, three-quarter-speed wind sprints of about 100 yards each. Then walk for about 50 yards before sprinting again. Have you ever noticed the legs on a sprinter? They are muscular, while a distance runner's legs have long and stringy muscles. Furthermore, long-distance jogging wreaks havoc with a pitcher's knees and lower back and should be avoided at all costs.

There you have it: a pitcher's primer for success. Armed with all the information in this book, any young, physically fit person can become, at the very least, a modestly successful pitcher. Remember, you cannot master all the pitches I've shown you here—no one can. Instead, pick and choose those pitches that suit your talents and work on them. Think of your career in terms of years, not games. Have patience; nothing worth having comes easily. Trust in yourself. Good luck!

You may never make it to the major leagues, but with practice, exercise, and the right attitude, you *can* be a winning pitcher.